Copyright 2024
Lloyd Culbertson
Published by Yaskey Productions. LLC
All rights reserved.

This book is designed to provide you with information for your understanding and knowledge. However, it should not be considered as medical advice. It is not intended to diagnose, treat, cure, or prevent any condition or disease. You must understand that this book is not a substitute for consultation with a licensed healthcare practitioner. We strongly recommend you consult your own physician or healthcare specialist regarding the suggestions and recommendations presented in this book. Your use of this book implies your acceptance of this disclaimer.

The publisher and the author want to make it clear that they do not guarantee the level of success that may be experienced by following the advice and strategies in this book. It's important to understand that results may vary for each individual. Furthermore, the publisher and the authorsmake no representations or warranties of any kind regarding this book or its contents. They disclaim all such representations and warranties, including, but not limited to, warranties of fitness for a particular purpose. Additionally, the publisher and the author assume no responsibility for errors, inaccuracies, omissions, or other inconsistencies.

Facing the Inevitable

The soft glow of the morning sun filtered through the curtains, casting a warm hue over the cozy living room where Sarah sat, her fingers poised over the keys of her laptop. With a furrowed brow and a deep sigh, she attempted to muster the focus needed to tackle her overflowing inbox. But today, like so many others lately, her mind was elsewhere, tethered to the unsettling reality unfolding before her eyes.

Across the room, her father, George, sat in his favorite armchair, a worn newspaper resting in his lap. His once sharp gaze now seemed clouded with confusion, and his wrinkled hands fumbled aimlessly with the pages. Sarah watched him silently, her heart heavy with a mixture of frustration and sorrow.

At eighty-two, George was entering a new chapter of his life marked by forgetfulness and uncertainty. Simple tasks that were once second nature now seemed insurmountable obstacles. Names slipped from his grasp like sand through his fingers, and the threads of conversation often unraveled before they could be woven into coherent thoughts.

As Sarah observed her father's struggle, a knot tightened in her chest, constricting her breath with each passing moment. She longed to reach out, to offer comfort and reassurance, but she found herself paralyzed by a potent cocktail of emotions—frustration, fear, and a gnawing sense of helplessness.

This scene, this delicate dance of love and loss, is becoming all too familiar in households across the globe. With each passing year, the population ages, and the specter of dementia looms ever larger on the horizon. Yet, despite its prevalence, the journey through aging and cognitive decline remains shrouded in silence and stigma.

Sarah's experience with her father was not unique. Countless families find themselves navigating the murky waters of aging, grappling with the profound challenges it presents. And yet, amidst the frustration and uncertainty, there existed a quiet resilience—a steadfast determination to weather the storm, no matter how fierce.

As Sarah pondered the complexities of her father's condition, a sense of clarity began to dawn. This was not a journey she had to undertake alone. Together, she and George would navigate the twists and turns of this unfamiliar terrain, drawing strength from the bonds of love and shared history that bound them together.

For all its trials and tribulations, the aging journey is a testament to the resilience of the human spirit—a reminder that even in the face of adversity, moments of profound beauty and connection exist. And as Sarah gazed upon her father, a gentle smile tugged at the corners of her lips, illuminating the room with a glimmer of hope.

Yes, the road ahead would be fraught with challenges, but they would face them together, one step at a time.

And so, as the morning sun cast its golden rays upon the world outside, Sarah took a deep breath, steeling herself for the journey ahead. In embracing uncertainty, she found the strength to carry on, guided by the unwavering love that bound her to her father. This love transcended the boundaries of time and space, illuminating the path forward with its radiant glow.

However, Sarah knew that while she had survived this day, tomorrow was on the way.

Recognizing the overwhelming weight of her emotions, Sarah realized the importance of seeking support and understanding from others who shared similar experiences. Turning to social media sites and online platforms, she discovered a wealth of virtual communities filled with empathy, compassion, and solidarity. In these digital spaces, she found refuge, where she could openly share her fears, doubts, and joys with others who understood the complexities of anticipatory grief. Surrounded by a network of compassionate souls, Sarah found solace in the collective wisdom and resilience of her online community, reminding her that she was never truly alone on this journey.

Echoes of Our Own Struggles

As Sarah grappled with the complexities of her father's aging, she couldn't help but feel the weight of her own emotions mirrored in the countless stories shared by others. In the quiet moments of solitude, she found herself drawn to the shared experiences of strangers—voices that echoed her own struggles and offered a glimmer of solace amid uncertainty.

Scrolling through her social media feed, Sarah stumbled upon a post that spoke directly to her heart. It was a simple yet poignant reflection on the challenges of watching loved ones grow older, resonating with a raw honesty that struck a chord deep within her soul.

The comments that followed were a testament to the universality of Sarah's experience. Stories poured forth from individuals of all walks of life—daughters, sons, spouses, and friends—each grappling with their own journey through the labyrinth of aging and loss.

Some shared tales of tender moments shared with aging parents, small gestures of love and kindness that illuminated the darkest of days. Others bared their souls, laying bare the rawness of grief and the ache of longing for a past that seemed forever out of reach.

Yet, amidst the sorrow and uncertainty, a thread of resilience existed—a quiet strength that bound them together in solidarity. In the face of adversity, they found solace in the shared understanding that they were not alone—that their struggles were echoed in the hearts of countless others who walked this path before them.

For Sarah, this realization was both comforting and humbling. In the depths of her despair, she had often felt isolated, adrift in a sea of uncertainty with no one to turn to for guidance. But now, surrounded by her virtual community's collective wisdom and compassion, she found herself buoyed by a renewed sense of hope.

As she read through the stories shared by her newfound companions, Sarah felt a sense of kinship—a recognition that their struggles were her struggles, their triumphs her triumphs. In their words, she found the courage to confront her fears and embrace the uncertainty of the journey ahead with a newfound sense of grace and resilience.

With a heart full of relief and a newfound sense of camaraderie, Sarah reflected on the profound realization that her struggles were not hers alone to bear. As she closed her laptop, she embraced the knowledge that her experience resonated with countless others navigating the complexities of aging and anticipatory grief. In the shared narratives of strangers turned allies, she found validation and solidarity, recognizing that her journey was part of a collective tapestry woven by generations of individuals facing similar trials and tribulations. With this newfound perspective, Sarah approached the challenges of her father's aging with a renewed sense of resilience and understanding, fortified by the knowledge that she was part of a larger community united by empathy and compassion.

Demographic Shifts: The Rising Tide of Aging in America

In addition to the shared experiences of individuals like Sarah, broader demographic trends underscore the increasing prevalence of aging and the challenges it presents. According to recent studies, the American population is aging at an unprecedented rate, driven by factors such as increased life expectancy and the aging of the baby boomer generation.

One study conducted by the U.S. Census Bureau projected that by the year 2030, all baby boomers will be older than age 65, meaning that one in every five Americans will be of retirement age. This demographic shift has significant implications for healthcare and social services, as a larger proportion of the population will require care and support in their later years.

Furthermore, as life expectancy continues to rise, so does the prevalence of age-related conditions such as Alzheimer's disease and other forms of dementia. A report by the Alzheimer's Association estimated that by 2050, the number of Americans living with Alzheimer's disease could nearly triple, reaching over 14 million individuals.

These projections paint a sobering picture of the future landscape of aging in America, highlighting the urgent need for policies and resources to support older adults and their families.

As Sarah navigates the challenges of caring for her aging father, she is not alone in her struggle. Across the country, millions of families are facing similar challenges, grappling with the complexities of aging and striving to provide the best possible care for their loved ones in the face of an uncertain future.

What Sarah may not realize is that what she is experiencing is a well-documented phenomenon known as anticipatory grief. Anticipatory grief refers to the mourning and emotional preparation that occurs when individuals confront the impending loss of a loved one. In Sarah's case, her feelings of sadness, anxiety, and fear regarding her father's declining health are all manifestations of anticipatory grief, a concept that will be explored in depth in the following chapters.

Navigating Anticipatory Grief with Compassion and Resilience

As we journey through life, we are inevitably confronted with moments of transition and change. For many, the process of aging—both for ourselves and for our loved ones—represents one of the most profound and challenging transitions we will face. In the face of uncertainty and loss, seeking comfort and guidance to navigate these uncharted waters is natural.

Offering a Safe Space for Reflection and Discussion

This book serves as a beacon of solace and support for those grappling with the complexities of anticipatory grief as they watch their aging parents navigate the twilight years of their lives. Within these pages, readers will find a safe space for reflection and discussion—a sanctuary where their fears, hopes, and uncertainties are not just met, but deeply understood and empathized with.

Through candid exploration and thoughtful reflection, readers are invited to confront the myriad emotions accompanying anticipatory grief. From the initial shock and denial to the eventual acceptance and adaptation, each stage of the grieving process is illuminated with compassion and insight. Readers will find solace in the knowledge that they are part of a community, not alone in their journey.

Practical Strategies for Coping with Anticipatory Grief

Beyond providing a space for reflection, this book offers practical strategies and coping mechanisms to help readers navigate the turbulent waters of anticipatory grief with grace and resilience. Drawing on evidence-based techniques and expert insights, readers will discover a wealth of resources to support them on their journey.

From mindfulness practices and relaxation techniques to communication strategies and self-care rituals, this book will find a toolbox of practical strategies to help navigate the challenges of caring for aging parents while tending to their own emotional well-being. Through gentle guidance and compassionate support, readers will learn to cultivate resilience in the face of adversity and find moments of peace and tranquility amidst the storm.

In addition to practical strategies, this book provides a roadmap for seeking support and finding outlets for expression. Whether through support groups, therapy, or creative outlets such as writing or art, readers will discover many ways to connect with others and process their emotions in healthy and constructive ways.

Ultimately, the purpose of this book is to provide comfort and guidance to those facing anticipatory grief with aging parents. By offering a safe space for reflection and discussion and providing practical strategies for coping with grief, this book aims to empower readers, giving them the tools and knowledge to navigate the challenges of caregiving with compassion, resilience, and grace.

Navigating Anticipatory Grief

Anticipatory grief is a multifaceted emotional experience that arises in response to the impending loss of a loved one. It encompasses a range of emotions, thoughts, and behaviors that individuals may undergo as they anticipate the eventual death of someone close to them. Unlike grief that occurs after a loss has occurred, anticipatory grief begins before the death and can continue for an extended period of time.

Anticipatory grief can be characterized by feelings of sadness, anxiety, anger, guilt, and a sense of loss. Individuals may find themselves preoccupied with thoughts of the impending loss, experiencing a heightened awareness of the finite nature of life and the inevitability of death. This preoccupation may lead to anticipatory mourning, where individuals begin to grieve the impending loss before it has actually occurred.

In the context of aging parents, anticipatory grief often manifests as a response to the decline in physical and cognitive functioning that comes with old age. Watching a parent struggle with memory loss, mobility issues, or chronic illness can trigger feelings of anticipatory grief as individuals grapple with the impending loss of their parent's health and vitality.

Acknowledging the Validity of Mixed Emotions Surrounding Aging Parents

The validity of the emotions experienced during anticipatory grief cannot be overstated. Grief is a profoundly personal and individual experience, and there is no right or wrong way to grieve. It is natural for individuals to experience a wide range of emotions as they confront the impending loss of a loved one.

Some common emotions experienced during anticipatory grief include:

- **Sadness:** Sadness is a natural response to the prospect of losing a loved one. It may arise from realizing that time with a loved one is limited and their presence will be greatly missed.
- **Anxiety:** Anxiety often accompanies anticipatory grief as individuals grapple with uncertainty about the future. Fear of the unknown, concerns about caregiving responsibilities,

and worries about how life will change after the loss may contribute to feelings of anxiety.

- **Anger:** Anger is a common response to grief and may arise from feelings of helplessness, frustration, or injustice. Individuals may feel angry at the situation, at themselves, or others involved in the caregiving process.
- **Guilt:** Guilt is a pervasive emotion in anticipatory grief and may stem from a variety of sources. Individuals may feel guilty for not spending enough time with their loved ones, for past conflicts or misunderstandings, or for feeling relief or ambivalence about the impending loss.

The Importance of Validating Feelings:

Validating feelings is not just a crucial step in grieving, it's a lifeline. Particularly when anticipating the loss of aging parents, it's easy to feel overwhelmed. But by suppressing or denying emotions, we only intensify them, leading to more significant distress. However, by acknowledging the validity of our mixed emotions, we can begin to cope with anticipatory grief with greater understanding and compassion. Validating feelings allows us to honor our experiences and create space for healing, bringing a much-needed sense of relief.

Practical Tips for Validating Feelings:

- **Self-Awareness:** A key aspect of validating feelings is self-awareness. It's important to take the time to recognize and acknowledge your own emotions surrounding the impending loss of aging parents. By allowing yourself to feel without judgment or criticism, you can cultivate a deeper understanding of your emotions. Journaling or mindfulness practices can be helpful tools in this process.
- **Active Listening:** When supporting others, practice active listening. Validate their emotions by reflecting back on what they are expressing without judgment. Use phrases like, "I hear you" or "That sounds really tough."

Active listening is not just a communication skill; it's a powerful tool for validating the emotions and experiences of others. This is particularly crucial when supporting elderly individuals through anticipatory grief. By fully engaging with and understanding what they are saying, we can go beyond simply hearing words. We can pay close attention to their words, tone, and body language, demonstrating empathy and understanding. This fosters a sense of connection and support that is invaluable during this challenging time.

When practicing active listening, focusing on the speaker and avoiding distractions is essential. Give them your full attention, maintain eye contact, and use verbal and nonverbal cues to show that you are engaged in the conversation. Reflect back on what the speaker is saying by paraphrasing their words and summarizing their feelings. This shows that you are truly listening and understanding their perspective.

Active listening is not just a skill, it's a powerful tool, especially for elderly individuals. Aging can bring about various challenges, such as hearing loss and cognitive decline, making communication more difficult. But active listening can bridge this gap, ensuring that their voices are heard and their feelings are validated. It empowers them to communicate effectively, despite the challenges they may face.

When communicating with elderly individuals who may have hearing or cognitive issues, it's essential to adjust your approach to active listening:

➤ **Speak Clearly and Slowly:** Enunciate your words clearly and speak at a moderate pace to make it easier for them to understand.

- **Use Simple Language:** Avoid using complex or technical language that may be difficult for them to grasp. Keep your sentences concise and straightforward.
- **Provide Visual Cues:** Use visual aids or gestures to reinforce your message and help them better understand what you're saying.
- **Patience is key when communicating with elderly individuals who may have hearing or cognitive issues.** Give them time to process information and respond. Avoid interrupting or finishing their sentences, as this can be frustrating and undermine their sense of autonomy. Your patience reassures them that their thoughts and feelings are valued.
- **Repeat and Clarify:** If necessary, repeat key points and clarify any misunderstandings. Break information into smaller chunks to make it more manageable.

By practicing active listening and adapting your communication style to accommodate the needs of elderly individuals, you can effectively support them through the challenges of anticipatory grief, validating their emotions and fostering a sense of connection and understanding.

- **Empathy:** Empathy is not just a concept, it's a crucial skill in personal relationships. It's the ability to understand and share another person's feelings. It involves putting yourself in someone else's shoes and imagining how they might be feeling in a particular situation. When practicing empathy, you strive to connect with the other person's emotions on a deep level, even if you haven't experienced exactly what they're going through. It's about recognizing and acknowledging their feelings as valid and offering support and understanding. By mastering empathy, you can enhance your relationships and make them more meaningful.

Empathy differs from sympathy because it goes beyond simply acknowledging someone else's emotions. While sympathy involves feeling sorry for someone or expressing pity, empathy involves actively engaging with their emotions and trying to understand their perspective. One way to develop empathy is to actively listen to others without judgment, and to ask open-ended questions to encourage them to share more. Instead of just offering condolences or reassurance from a distance, empathy requires a deeper level of emotional connection and understanding.

For example, if a friend is grieving the loss of a loved one, sympathy might involve saying something like, "I'm sorry for your loss." While this statement is well-intentioned, it doesn't necessarily convey a proper understanding of the person's emotions. On the other hand, empathy might involve saying something like, "I can't imagine how difficult this must be for you. I'm here for you if you need to talk or if there's anything I can do to support you."

Empathy is genuinely listening to and validating someone else's feelings, even if you haven't experienced the same situation. It's a powerful tool for building connections and offering meaningful support to those who are grieving or facing difficult emotions. By practicing empathy, you cannot only strengthen your relationships but also foster personal growth by gaining a deeper understanding of others and the world around you.

- **Normalize Feelings:** As healthcare worker, your role in normalizing feelings is crucial in supporting individuals experiencing anticipatory grief. It involves acknowledging and accepting the wide range of emotions that people may go through during this challenging time. One crucial aspect of normalizing feelings is emphasizing that there is no right or wrong way to feel.

In anticipatory grief, individuals may experience a myriad of emotions, including sadness, anger, guilt, anxiety, and even relief. These feelings can be complex and may fluctuate over time. By normalizing these emotions, we validate the person's experiences and reassure them that their feelings are valid and understandable given the circumstances.

However, the concept of "normal" can be challenging to define in the context of grief. For instance, feeling sad or anxious is often considered a typical emotional response. Yet, what may seem like a typical emotional response for one person, such as feeling relief, may be entirely different for another. Cultural background, personality, and past experiences can all influence how someone processes and expresses their emotions.

Therefore, avoiding labeling certain feelings as abnormal or invalid is essential. Instead, we should empower individuals to express themselves authentically and without judgment. By creating a safe and accepting environment for emotional expression, we help individuals feel understood and supported in their grief journey.

Additionally, normalizing feelings can help reduce feelings of isolation and loneliness. When individuals realize that others, including healthcare professionals, are going through similar emotions, they may feel less alone in their experiences. This sense of shared humanity can be comforting and reassuring, fostering a sense of connection and solidarity among those experiencing anticipatory grief.

Normalizing feelings is a compassionate and validating way to support individuals as they navigate the complexities of anticipatory grief. By normalizing feelings of others, we acknowledge the legitimacy of their emotions and emphasize that there is no right or wrong way to feel. This is different from validating feelings, which involves accepting and understanding the person's emotions, even if we don't agree with them. By normalizing and validating feelings, we can help individuals feel seen, heard, and understood during this challenging time.

- **Encourage Expression:** Expression through art and creative outlets can provide individuals with alternative ways to explore and process emotions. Here are some examples of how art and creative activities can be used to facilitate expression:

➢ **Painting or Drawing**: Encourage individuals to express their emotions through painting or drawing. For instance, one might paint a vibrant sunset to symbolize the beauty and fleeting nature of life or draw a portrait of their loved one to capture their essence. Putting a brush on canvas or a pencil on paper can be cathartic and therapeutic, allowing for a tangible representation of their emotions.

➢ **Journaling**: Suggest keeping a journal to record thoughts, feelings, and reflections on anticipatory grief. This personal and private outlet for expression can be a comforting companion during difficult times. Writing can serve as a structured and reflective manner to explore emotions. Prompts or guided journaling exercises can help stimulate reflection and insight, offering a sense of understanding and respect for one's unique journey.

➢ **Music and Songwriting**: Listening to music or composing songs can be a powerful means of emotional expression. Encourage individuals to create playlists of songs that resonate with their feelings or to write and perform their own music. This creative process can be empowering, allowing individuals to convey complex emotions and experiences in a way that words alone sometimes cannot. It's a reminder of their strength and capability.

➤ **Photography**: Photography offers a visual medium for individuals to capture and explore their emotions. Encourage individuals to take photographs that symbolize their experiences of anticipatory grief or to create photo collages that tell a story of their journey. Framing and composing images can provide a sense of control and perspective.

➤ **Sculpture or Crafts**: Working with clay, wood, or other materials can be a tactile and hands-on way to express emotions. Encourage individuals to create sculptures or crafts that symbolize their feelings or represent aspects of their relationship with their aging parents. If you're new to this, start with simple crafts like origami or knitting. The process of shaping and molding materials can be both therapeutic and empowering, but it's important to remember that it's the process, not the end result, that matters.

➢ **Dance or Movement**: Movement-based activities like dance or yoga can help individuals connect with their bodies and release pent-up emotions. Encourage individuals to engage in expressive movement practices that allow them to embody their feelings and experiences physically. This might involve freestyle dance, guided movement meditations, or yoga sequences focused on emotional release.

By encouraging individuals to explore these creative outlets, we provide them with opportunities to express themselves in ways that resonate with their unique preferences and experiences. However, it's important to note that these activities are most effective when done in conjunction with professional guidance or support. Creative expression can be a powerful tool for processing emotions, gaining insight, and finding solace during anticipatory grief, but it's crucial to have someone who can help navigate through these emotions.

Consequences of Invalidating Feelings:

Invalidating or ignoring feelings can have significant negative consequences on an individual's emotional well-being and ability to cope with grief. Here's an expanded look at the impact of invalidation, including examples of what it might look like in practice:

- **Feelings of Misunderstanding and Isolation**: When emotions are dismissed or invalidated, individuals may feel their experiences are not being recognized or understood. This can lead to feelings of loneliness and isolation, as they may struggle to find validation and support for their emotions. Individuals may feel disconnected from those around them without acknowledgment, exacerbating their sense of isolation. Empathy plays a crucial role in validating emotions:
- **Shame and Self-Doubt**: Invalidating responses can evoke feelings of shame or self-doubt in individuals. They may question the validity of their emotions, wondering if they are overreacting or being unreasonable. This self-doubt can erode their self-esteem and confidence, making it even more challenging to navigate the grieving process.
- **Emotional Distress and Avoidance**: Invalidating or ignoring feelings can contribute to heightened emotional distress. Individuals may suppress their emotions or avoid discussing them altogether in an attempt to avoid further invalidation. However, suppressing emotions can lead to

31

increased psychological distress and may prolong the grieving process. Unaddressed emotions may resurface later, potentially intensifying in intensity. The long-term effects of invalidation on emotional well-being and the grieving process can be significant:

- **Strained Relationships**: Invalidation can strain relationships, creating a disconnect between individuals. When feelings are dismissed, it can erode trust and intimacy in relationships, making it difficult for individuals to feel emotionally supported by those closest to them. This is a pressing issue that needs to be addressed, as over time, repeated invalidation may damage the foundation of a relationship, leading to resentment and distance.

- **Barriers to Effective Communication and Support**: Invalidating responses can create barriers to effective communication and support. However, by fostering empathy and understanding, we can break down these barriers. When individuals feel their emotions are valued and respected, they are more likely to open up and seek help when needed. This open communication is crucial in the grieving process, as it allows individuals to access the support they need to cope with their emotions effectively.

Overall, invalidating or ignoring feelings can have profound and long-lasting effects on an individual's emotional well-being and ability to navigate the grieving process. It's essential to recognize the importance of validating emotions and creating a supportive environment where individuals feel heard, understood, and valued in their experiences of grief and loss.

Conclusion: In navigating anticipatory grief, validating feelings is essential for promoting understanding, compassion, and healing. By acknowledging the validity of emotions, individuals can honor their experiences and find resilience in the face of loss. Practicing self-awareness, active listening, empathy, and normalization of feelings can facilitate the validation process. Conversely, invalidating feelings can prolong distress and hinder the grieving process.

Understanding Aging as a Natural and Universal Experience

Aging, an intrinsic and universal facet of the human condition, unfurls as a gradual tapestry of transformations spanning the physical, cognitive, and social realms. From the moment of birth, each individual embarks on a journey inexorably marked by the passage of time, traversing through the various stages of life with aging as an ever-present companion.

The U.S. Census Bureau's statistical insights offer a snapshot of this societal shift. In 2020, the demographic landscape unveiled a striking reality: adults aged 65 and above constituted 16.5% of the nation's populace. Yet projections unfurl an even more resounding narrative, forecasting an escalation in this demographic's presence. By the dawn of the 2030s, an estimated one in every five Americans will have reached the retirement age threshold. This surge underscores the pervasive influence of aging, permeating the very fabric of society.

Within the intricate tapestry of aging lies a multitude of physiological transformations that weave together to define the journey of growing older. Muscles, once resilient and robust, gradually undergo a process of atrophy, experiencing a reduction in both mass and strength as the years pass by. This decline in muscle mass, known as sarcopenia, contributes to a gradual loss of mobility and functional capacity in older adults. Concurrently, the skeletal system, once a stalwart fortress of support, undergoes a gradual deterioration of bone density, making bones more fragile and prone to fractures. This decline in bone density, known as osteoporosis, poses a significant risk to older adults, increasing their susceptibility to fractures and injuries, particularly in weight-bearing areas such as the hips and spine.

Moreover, the aging process impacts sensory perception, diminishing the acuity of once-sharp senses. Vision, once keen and acute, begins to falter as the lenses of the eyes lose elasticity and the retina undergoes structural changes. This can result in a decline in visual acuity, making it more difficult for older adults to see clearly, especially in low-light conditions. Similarly, hearing may become impaired as the delicate structures of the inner ear degenerate over time, leading to difficulties in discerning sounds and understanding speech. Taste and smell may also diminish, as the sensory receptors responsible for detecting flavors and odors become less sensitive with age.

As the body undergoes these intricate changes, older adults may find themselves navigating a landscape transformed by the passage of time. Yet, amidst these physiological metamorphoses, there remains an enduring resilience and vitality that characterizes the human spirit, guiding individuals through the journey of aging with grace and resilience.

But the canvas of aging extends beyond the human realm, delving into the recesses of cognition and mental acuity. Memory, that tapestry of lived experiences, begins to fray at the edges, snippets of recollections slipping through the sieve of time. Research conducted by the National Institute on Aging (NIA) has revealed that age-related memory decline is a common phenomenon among older adults. According to their findings, older adults may experience changes in memory function, particularly in episodic memory, which involves the ability to recall specific events or experiences. A longitudinal study published in the journal Psychology and Aging found that older adults demonstrated declines in episodic memory over time, with performance decreasing by approximately 10% every decade after the age of 50.

Furthermore, once nimble and agile, processing speed slows to a languid pace, thoughts unfolding in measured cadence. The impact of aging on cognitive processing speed has been extensively studied, with research indicating that older adults typically exhibit slower processing speeds compared to younger individuals. A meta-analysis published in the journal Aging, Neuropsychology, and Cognition found that processing speed declines with age, with older adults showing slower reaction times and processing rates compared to their younger counterparts. This slowing of cognitive processing speed can have significant implications for daily functioning and may contribute to difficulties in tasks requiring quick decision-making and information processing.

As the canvas of aging unfurls, it becomes evident that cognitive changes are an integral part of the aging process. Yet, amidst these challenges, there remains a remarkable resilience and adaptability within the human mind, allowing individuals to navigate the complexities of aging with resilience.

Through a nuanced understanding of aging as a natural and universal experience, individuals can navigate the complexities of the aging process with grace and fortitude. Armed with knowledge and empathy, it is possible to traverse the winding pathways of life's journey, embracing each stage with reverence and resilience.

Exploring Society's Attitudes and Stigmas Toward Aging

Despite the universality of aging, societal attitudes and stigmas toward older adults often perpetuate negative stereotypes and misconceptions, casting a shadow over the lived experiences of seniors. Ageism, defined as systematic stereotyping, prejudice, and discrimination against individuals or groups based on their age, manifests in subtle and overt ways, shaping societal perceptions and interactions with older individuals. According to a report by the World Health Organization (WHO), ageism is pervasive across various sectors of society, including healthcare, employment, and media representation. It's crucial to note that ageism not only affects older adults' psychological well-being but also has tangible effects on their physical health outcomes, such as increased risk of chronic conditions and decreased life expectancy. This underscores the severity of the issue and the need for change.

Research conducted by the American Psychological Association (APA) revealed that ageism can have detrimental effects on older adults' mental and physical health. Older adults who experience ageism may internalize negative stereotypes about aging, leading to feelings of self-doubt, low self-esteem, and depression. Moreover, ageism can also influence healthcare providers' perceptions and treatment of older patients, leading to disparities in care and outcomes. A study published in the Journal of the American Geriatrics Society found that older adults who experienced ageism were less likely to receive appropriate medical treatment and preventive care compared to their younger counterparts.

Furthermore, ageism in the workplace contributes significantly to economic inequalities and barriers to employment for older adults, perpetuating a cycle of financial insecurity and social isolation. A comprehensive study conducted by the AARP, titled "The Value of Experience: AARP Multicultural Work and Jobs Study," sheds light on the prevalence and impact of age discrimination in hiring practices. According to the study, nearly two-thirds (64%) of workers aged 45 and older reported witnessing or experiencing age discrimination in the workplace. This discrimination manifests in various forms, including biased hiring practices, lack of promotional opportunities, and unfair treatment in the workplace.

The study further highlights the challenges faced by older job seekers in securing employment opportunities. Despite their wealth of experience and expertise, older adults often encounter age-related biases during the job search process, resulting in fewer job offers and longer periods of unemployment. Statistics from the study indicate that older job seekers are unemployed for an average of 55 weeks, compared to 34 weeks for younger job seekers. This prolonged unemployment not only exacerbates financial insecurity but also contributes to feelings of social isolation and diminished self-worth among older adults.

Moreover, age discrimination in the workplace has long-term financial implications for older adults, impacting their retirement savings and financial well-being. According to the AARP study, older workers who experience age discrimination are more likely to withdraw from the labor force prematurely, leading to reduced earnings and diminished retirement savings. This exacerbates the retirement savings gap and increases older adults' reliance on social security benefits and other forms of assistance in their later years.

Overall, the pervasive nature of age discrimination in the workplace has far-reaching consequences for older adults' economic security and well-being. Addressing ageism in hiring practices and promoting age-inclusive workplaces are essential steps towards creating a more equitable and supportive environment for older workers. By recognizing the value of older adults' skills and contributions, we can harness the full potential of our aging workforce and foster greater economic opportunity and social inclusion for people of all ages.

As society continues to grapple with the challenges of aging populations, addressing ageism becomes increasingly imperative. By challenging and rejecting stereotypes, promoting intergenerational understanding, and advocating for policies that promote inclusivity and respect for older adults, we can work towards creating a more equitable and age-friendly society for people of all ages.

Physical and Mental Impact of Ageism

Research conducted by the World Health Organization (WHO) provides compelling evidence of the detrimental impact of ageism on the physical and mental well-being of older adults. In a comprehensive study titled "Global Report on Ageism," the WHO highlighted how negative stereotypes about aging permeate cultural narratives around the world, portraying older adults as frail, dependent, and burdensome. These stereotypes not only erode the dignity and autonomy of older individuals but also contribute to the perpetuation of ageist attitudes and behaviors within society.

The study further emphasizes how cultural attitudes towards aging vary significantly across different regions and societies, reflecting diverse perspectives on the role and value of older adults within communities. In some cultures, older adults are revered and respected for their wisdom, experience, and contributions to the fabric of society. This positive view of aging, as seen in many Asian cultures like Japan and China, where older adults are often regarded as the guardians of tradition and custodians of cultural heritage, can inspire us to foster similar attitudes in our own societies. Similarly, Indigenous communities around the world, including those in Africa, Latin America, and Australia, hold elders in high regard, valuing their knowledge, leadership, and spiritual guidance within the community. This reverence for elders, their connection to ancestral wisdom, and their integral role in maintaining their communities' cultural identity and cohesion can serve as a beacon of hope for a more inclusive and respectful future for older adults.

Conversely, in other cultures, ageist beliefs and stereotypes may prevail, contributing to the marginalization and discrimination of older adults. In Western societies, including the United States and European countries, ageism often manifests in media representations and societal attitudes that portray aging as a process of decline and deterioration. Negative stereotypes depict older individuals as frail, dependent, and burdensome, perpetuating ageist attitudes and behaviors within society. This can lead to age-based discrimination in various domains, including employment, healthcare, and social services. Older adults may encounter barriers to employment opportunities due to age-related biases in hiring practices, experience disparities in healthcare access and treatment, and face challenges in accessing social support and resources. The prevalence of ageism in Western societies exacerbates the challenges faced by older adults and undermines their dignity, autonomy, and quality of life.

Addressing ageism requires a concerted effort, a collective responsibility, to challenge stereotypes, promote intergenerational understanding, and foster inclusive attitudes towards aging across cultures. By recognizing and valuing the contributions of older adults, societies can create environments that honor the wisdom, experience, and resilience of older individuals, fostering greater social inclusion and well-being for people of all ages. Efforts to combat ageism must be culturally sensitive and responsive to the diverse attitudes and beliefs surrounding aging, promoting respect, dignity, and equity for older adults in all societies. This collective action, this shared responsibility, can empower us to make a real difference in the lives of older adults, and in turn, in the fabric of our societies.

These profoundly ingrained attitudes can have far-reaching consequences, significantly influencing healthcare providers' perceptions and treatment of older patients. Studies conducted by reputable organizations such as the World Health Organization (WHO) have shed light on the detrimental impact of ageism within healthcare settings. The WHO's report, "Global Report on Ageism," underscores how ageist beliefs and stereotypes can lead to disparities in care, contributing to substandard treatment and poorer health outcomes among older adults.

Statistics from the WHO report reveal alarming disparities in healthcare access and treatment based on age. Older adults may encounter age-based biases and discrimination when seeking medical care, resulting in delayed diagnosis, inadequate treatment, and decreased adherence to medical recommendations. For example, a study published in the Journal of the American Geriatrics Society found that older adults with acute myocardial infarction (heart attack) were less likely to receive invasive cardiac procedures such as angioplasty or coronary artery bypass surgery compared to younger patients despite having similar clinical indications. This disparity in treatment may stem from ageist assumptions about older adults' ability to tolerate and benefit from medical interventions, leading to underutilization of potentially life-saving treatments.

Furthermore, ageist attitudes can influence healthcare providers' communication and decision-making processes when caring for older patients. Older adults may encounter age-related biases in the provision of pain management, with healthcare providers underestimating or dismissing their pain symptoms based on ageist stereotypes about pain tolerance in older individuals. This can result in undertreatment of pain and decreased quality of life for older adults. Additionally, ageism may contribute to the underdiagnosis and undertreatment of mental health conditions in older adults, perpetuating stigma and barriers to accessing appropriate care.

Addressing ageism within healthcare requires a multifaceted approach encompassing education, training, and policy initiatives to promote age-inclusive practices and mitigate the impact of age-based biases on patient care. By raising awareness of ageism and its consequences among healthcare providers, fostering empathy and cultural competence, and implementing guidelines for age-appropriate care, we can work towards creating healthcare environments that prioritize dignity, respect, and equitable treatment for patients of all ages.

Efforts to combat ageism and promote positive attitudes toward aging are crucial for cultivating a society that values and respects individuals of all ages. Intergenerational programs, which facilitate meaningful interactions between older adults and younger generations, serve to challenge stereotypes and foster empathy and understanding across age groups.

Public education campaigns are vital in challenging ageist narratives and promoting a culture of inclusivity and respect for older adults. By highlighting seniors' diverse experiences and contributions, these campaigns seek to dismantle stereotypes and foster a more nuanced understanding of aging.

Policies that promote inclusivity and accessibility for older adults are also essential for creating age-friendly communities. From accessible public transportation to affordable housing options, these policies help older adults maintain their independence and autonomy, enabling them to live fulfilling and dignified lives.

By understanding aging as a natural and universal experience and actively challenging societal attitudes and stigmas toward older adults, individuals can cultivate empathy, compassion, and appreciation for aging.

Embracing life's inevitable changes with openness and understanding can foster a culture of respect and dignity for individuals of all ages, ensuring that every stage of life is valued and celebrated.

Navigating the Emotional Landscape of Anticipatory Grief

Defining Anticipatory Grief:
What Is It and How Does It Manifest?

It's essential to acknowledge the emotional complexity inherent in anticipating loss. Anticipatory grief, a phenomenon often overlooked in discussions of loss and grief, represents a multifaceted emotional experience that arises in response to the impending loss of a loved one. Unlike grief that occurs after the actual loss, anticipatory grief begins before death and can persist for an extended period.

At its core, anticipatory grief encompasses a wide spectrum of emotions, each as intricate and nuanced as the next. From the initial shock and disbelief upon learning of a loved one's terminal diagnosis to the profound sadness and longing that ensue as the inevitability of loss looms closer, individuals grappling with anticipatory grief navigate through a kaleidoscope of emotions. These emotions may fluctuate unpredictably, with individuals experiencing periods of intense sorrow, anger, guilt, anxiety, and even relief.

It's essential to recognize that the emotional responses to anticipatory grief vary from person to person, and there is no one-size-fits-all experience. Some individuals may find themselves consumed by sadness and despair, while others may experience a sense of emotional numbness or detachment as a coping mechanism. Additionally, conflicting emotions such as relief or guilt may arise, particularly in situations where the loved one's illness has caused prolonged suffering.

No emotional response to anticipatory grief is wrong or invalid. Each individual's journey through anticipatory grief is unique, shaped by their relationship with the dying person, their past experiences with loss, and their coping mechanisms. By acknowledging and validating the range of emotions experienced during anticipatory grief, individuals can begin to navigate this challenging process with greater understanding, compassion, and self-awareness.

Understanding the Cognitive and Behavioral Responses to Anticipatory Grief

In addition to emotional turmoil, anticipatory grief can also trigger a range of cognitive and behavioral responses that profoundly affect individuals' daily functioning. Research conducted by Bonanno and colleagues (2005) found that anticipatory grief is associated with heightened levels of intrusive thoughts and rumination about the impending loss. These rumination tendencies can lead to feelings of anxiety, uncertainty, and a pervasive sense of impending doom as individuals grapple with the anticipation of their loved one's death.

Moreover, studies have shown that anticipatory grief can significantly disrupt individuals' cognitive processes, impacting their ability to concentrate and make decisions. A study by Kissane and colleagues (2014) revealed that individuals experiencing anticipatory grief often report difficulties in maintaining attention and processing information, which can impair their performance in daily tasks and responsibilities.

Behaviorally, individuals may change their daily routines and habits to cope with the impending loss. Sleep disturbances, including insomnia and fragmented sleep patterns, are commonly reported symptoms of anticipatory grief. A study published in the Journal of Palliative Medicine by Nielsen and colleagues (2017) found that caregivers experiencing anticipatory grief frequently struggle with sleep disturbances, with disruptions in sleep quality impacting their overall well-being and functioning.

Additionally, appetite changes are common manifestations of anticipatory grief, with individuals experiencing fluctuations in appetite and eating patterns. A study by Hall and colleagues (2016) found that caregivers facing anticipatory grief often report changes in appetite, including decreased appetite and weight loss, as well as increased cravings for comfort foods as a coping mechanism.

Overall, the cognitive and behavioral responses to anticipatory grief highlight the profound impact of grief on both the mind and body. By understanding these responses and their underlying mechanisms, individuals can better recognize and cope with the challenges of anticipatory grief, seeking support and resources to navigate this complex emotional journey.

Recognizing the Signs: Emotional, Physical, and Psychological Responses

As individuals navigate the emotional landscape of anticipatory grief, it is crucial to recognize the signs and symptoms that may accompany this complex process. Numerous studies and clinical observations have shed light on individuals' diverse experiences during anticipatory grief, highlighting the need for comprehensive support and understanding.

Emotional responses such as sadness, anger, guilt, and anxiety are among the most common manifestations of anticipatory grief. A study by Prigerson and colleagues (2003) found that caregivers facing the impending loss of a loved one reported high levels of emotional distress, including feelings of sadness and anxiety. These emotions often fluctuate unpredictably, intensifying during moments of reflection or when confronted with reminders of the impending loss. Moreover, research by Stroebe and Schut (2001) suggests that feelings of guilt and self-blame are prevalent among individuals experiencing anticipatory grief, particularly if they perceive themselves as unable to alleviate their loved one's suffering.

Physically, individuals may experience a variety of symptoms that reflect the toll of anticipatory grief on the body. Studies have shown that caregivers and family members facing anticipatory grief frequently report symptoms such as fatigue, lethargy, headaches, and gastrointestinal distress. A study published in the Journal of Pain and Symptom Management by Nielsen and colleagues (2018) found that caregivers experiencing anticipatory grief had higher rates of physical symptoms compared to non-caregivers, indicating the profound impact of grief on physical well-being.

Psychologically, individuals may struggle with a myriad of feelings that compound the emotional and physical symptoms of anticipatory grief. Feelings of helplessness, hopelessness, and a diminished sense of self-worth are common psychological responses to anticipatory grief. Research by Maciejewski and colleagues (2007) suggests that individuals experiencing anticipatory grief may grapple with existential concerns, questioning the meaning and purpose of life in the face of impending loss.

Recognizing and addressing these multifaceted signs and symptoms of anticipatory grief is essential for supporting individuals as they navigate this challenging emotional journey. By providing comprehensive support and resources tailored to the unique needs of those experiencing anticipatory grief, healthcare providers and caregivers can help alleviate distress and promote coping strategies that foster resilience and well-being.

Recognizing the Signs: Emotional, Physical, and Psychological Responses

Emotional Responses: Sadness, Anxiety, Anger, Guilt

Emotional responses play a central role in the experience of anticipatory grief, reflecting the profound sense of loss and impending separation that individuals grapple with as they anticipate the death of a loved one. Sadness permeates the emotional landscape, a poignant reminder of the impending void that will be left in the wake of the loss. Anxiety casts a shadow over the horizon, fueled by uncertainty about the future and fears of what lies ahead. Anger may surface as individuals struggle to make sense of their emotions, directing their frustration toward themselves, others, or even the situation itself. Guilt, a common companion of grief, may arise as individuals wrestle with feelings of responsibility or regret, questioning whether they could have done more to prevent the impending loss.

Physical Symptoms: Fatigue, Sleep Disturbances, and Appetite Changes

The physical toll of anticipatory grief can be profound, manifesting in a variety of symptoms that impact individuals' day-to-day functioning. Fatigue weighs heavy on the body, a constant companion that saps energy and drains vitality. Sleep disturbances disrupt the natural rhythms of rest and rejuvenation, leaving individuals feeling weary and worn. Appetite changes may also occur, with some individuals experiencing a loss of appetite while others may turn to food for comfort in their distress. These physical symptoms not only exacerbate the emotional distress of anticipatory grief but can also impact individuals' overall health and well-being.

Psychological Impact: Cognitive Distortions and Existential Concerns

In addition to the emotional and physical symptoms, anticipatory grief can profoundly impact individuals' psychological well-being, giving rise to cognitive distortions and existential concerns that further complicate the grieving process. Cognitive distortions, recognized as standard features of grief, can exacerbate emotional distress and impede coping efforts. These distortions may include black-and-white thinking, where individuals view situations in extremes without considering nuances or possibilities; catastrophizing, where they magnify the potential adverse outcomes of a situation; and overgeneralization, where they draw broad conclusions based on limited evidence.

Studies have shown that cognitive distortions are prevalent among individuals experiencing anticipatory grief. For example, a study by Eisma and Stroebe (2017) found that caregivers facing the impending loss of a loved one often engaged in cognitive distortions such as catastrophizing, leading to heightened levels of anxiety and distress. Similarly, research by Maciejewski and colleagues (2007) highlighted the role of cognitive distortions in prolonging grief and complicating the grieving process, emphasizing the importance of addressing these distortions in grief therapy interventions.

Existential concerns, rooted in the fundamental questions of life, death, and meaning, may also emerge during anticipatory grief. As individuals confront the existential reality of mortality, they may grapple with profound questions about the purpose and meaning of life. These existential concerns can provoke feelings of existential angst, a profound sense of unease, and uncertainty about life's ultimate meaning and purpose. Research by Burke (2015) found that individuals experiencing anticipatory grief often reported heightened levels of existential distress, reflecting their struggle to find meaning and coherence in the face of impending loss.

Addressing cognitive distortions and existential concerns is essential for supporting individuals experiencing anticipatory grief. Therapeutic interventions such as cognitive-behavioral therapy (CBT) and existential therapy can help individuals challenge distorted thinking patterns and explore existential themes, facilitating a sense of acceptance, meaning-making, and existential resolution in the grieving process. By addressing these psychological aspects of anticipatory grief, healthcare providers and therapists can help individuals navigate the complexities of grief with greater resilience and understanding.

By recognizing the signs and symptoms of anticipatory grief, individuals can begin to navigate this complex emotional landscape with greater awareness and understanding. This journey is not one that needs to be faced alone. Through self-care practices, such as mindfulness and self-compassion, support from loved ones, and professional guidance, individuals can find comfort and solace amidst the uncertainty of anticipating loss.

The Role of Attachment:
Exploring the Deep Bonds with Aging Parents

Understanding the Unique Parent-Child Relationship

The parent-child relationship, widely regarded as one of the fundamental aspects of human experience, encapsulates a profound and enduring bond that transcends time and circumstance. It is a unique relationship characterized by unconditional love, nurturance, and mutual dependence, serving as a cornerstone for emotional development and familial cohesion. From the earliest stages of life, parents assume the role of caregivers, offering unwavering support, guidance, and protection as their children navigate the complexities of existence. This bond, forged in the crucible of shared experiences and mutual affection, deepens over time, evolving into a steadfast source of comfort and stability as individuals traverse the vicissitudes of adulthood.

Extensive research underscores the pivotal role of the parent-child relationship in shaping emotional development and overall well-being across the lifespan. A seminal study published in the Journal of Marriage and Family, for example, revealed how the quality of the parent-child relationship during adolescence can significantly predict psychological well-being in adulthood. This study underscored the enduring impact of early attachment experiences, highlighting the profound influence of parental care and support on long-term emotional resilience and adaptive functioning.

As parents age and transition into the later stages of life, the dynamics of the parent-child relationship inevitably undergo profound transformations. Adult children often grapple with the complexities of assuming caregiving roles for their aging parents, thereby reversing the traditional roles of dependence and care. These evolving dynamics can evoke a spectrum of emotions within adult children, ranging from feelings of responsibility and obligation to a poignant longing for the intimacy and closeness that characterized earlier stages of the parent-child relationship. The shifting sands of time necessitate a renegotiation of roles and expectations, challenging adult children to navigate the delicate balance between preserving their parents' autonomy and ensuring their well-being in the face of age-related vulnerabilities.

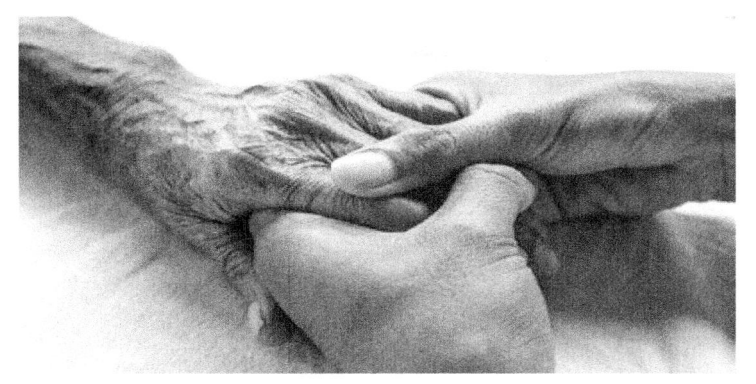

The Influence of Attachment Styles on Grief Response

Attachment theory, pioneered by psychologist John Bowlby, posits that individuals develop internal working attachment models based on their early experiences with caregivers. These internal working models shape individuals' beliefs and expectations about relationships, influencing their emotional responses to loss and separation.

Research has identified four primary attachment styles—secure, anxious-preoccupied, dismissive-avoidant, and fearful-avoidant—that individuals may exhibit in their relationships with others.

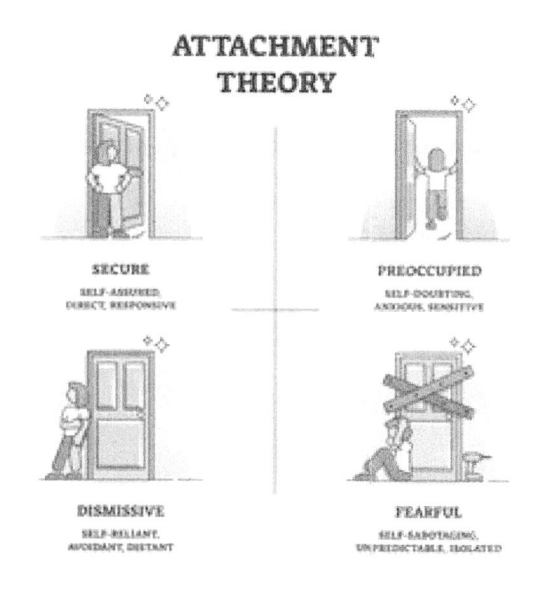

ATTACHMENT THEORY

SECURE
SELF-ASSURED,
DIRECT, RESPONSIVE

PREOCCUPIED
SELF-DOUBTING,
ANXIOUS, SENSITIVE

DISMISSIVE
SELF-RELIANT,
AVOIDANT, DISTANT

FEARFUL
SELF-SABOTAGING,
UNPREDICTABLE, ISOLATED

- **Secure Attachment**

Secure attachment lays the foundation for healthy and fulfilling relationships, including the parent-child relationship. Individuals with a secure attachment style often experience a strong sense of trust and security in their connections with others, including their parents. In the parent-child relationship, a secure attachment style fosters an environment of warmth, responsiveness, and emotional attunement. Children who develop a secure attachment with their parents feel comfortable expressing their needs and emotions openly, knowing their parents will respond with sensitivity and support.

Securely attached individuals tend to have positive internal working models of relationships, which shape their expectations and behaviors in future relationships, including romantic partnerships. This positive framework enables them to navigate conflicts and challenges constructively, as they trust in their ability to communicate effectively and resolve issues together. Moreover, individuals with a secure attachment style often exhibit higher levels of emotional intelligence, empathy, and resilience, contributing to their relationships' overall strength and longevity.

In the parent-child relationship, a secure attachment style not only strengthens the bond between parent and child but also paves the way for the child's social and emotional growth. Children who feel securely attached to their parents are more likely to develop a robust sense of self-esteem, autonomy, and interpersonal skills. They learn to regulate their emotions, form positive relationships with others, and explore the world with confidence and curiosity. This foundation of secure attachment sets the stage for the child's future relationships and overall development, highlighting its long-term benefits.

Secure attachment in the parent-child relationship creates a nurturing and supportive environment where children can thrive and flourish. It not only strengthens the parent-child bond but also enhances emotional well-being, setting the stage for the child's future relationships and overall development. This underscores the profound impact of secure attachment, encouraging parents to prioritize and invest in this bond.

- **Anxious-preoccupied attachment**

Individuals with an anxious-preoccupied attachment style tend to bring their relational anxieties into their parent-child relationships, impacting both their own experiences and those of their children. In the parent-child dynamic, these individuals may exhibit heightened sensitivity to perceived threats of rejection or abandonment from their parents, leading to a persistent need for reassurance and validation. Children of parents with an anxious-preoccupied attachment style may internalize their caregivers' anxieties, feeling responsible for meeting their parents' emotional needs and striving to earn their approval.

For individuals with an anxious-preoccupied attachment style, the parent-child relationship is a complex interplay of constant craving for closeness and validation, coupled with a deep-seated fear of rejection or abandonment. These individuals often struggle with feelings of insecurity and self-doubt, seeking constant reassurance from their parents to alleviate their anxieties. This reliance on external validation can create a pattern of clinginess or neediness in the parent-child relationship, as the anxious-preoccupied individual seeks constant affirmation of their worth and their lovability. Understanding and empathy towards these individuals are crucial for fostering a more secure and balanced relationship.

The anxious-preoccupied attachment style can manifest in various ways within the parent-child relationship, influencing both the parent's behavior and the child's experience. Parents with this attachment style may exhibit overprotective or controlling tendencies, striving to maintain a sense of closeness and connection with their child while simultaneously fearing rejection or abandonment. This can result in smothering behaviors or an inability to set appropriate boundaries, which may hinder the child's emotional development and autonomy.

Children of parents with an anxious-preoccupied attachment style may internalize their parents' anxieties, leading to feelings of guilt or responsibility for their parents' emotional well-being. These children may adapt by becoming overly compliant or seeking to soothe their parents' anxieties, sacrificing their needs. Additionally, they may struggle with feelings of inadequacy or self-doubt as they internalize their parents' fears of rejection or abandonment.

While the anxious-preoccupied attachment style can present challenges within the parent-child relationship, it also holds the potential for growth and improvement. Both parties, grappling with feelings of insecurity and dependency, can work towards a healthier and more balanced dynamic. This dynamic, characterized by mutual respect, trust, and emotional security, is not only possible but also within reach with recognition and addressing of these patterns.

- **Dismissive-avoidant attachment**

Individuals with a dismissive-avoidant attachment style bring their tendencies toward independence and emotional avoidance into their parent-child relationships, shaping the dynamics and interactions between parent and child. In the parent-child dynamic, these individuals may prioritize their autonomy and independence, leading them to downplay the importance of emotional closeness and connection with their parents. As a result, children of parents with a dismissive-avoidant attachment style may perceive their parents as emotionally distant or aloof, struggling to form deep, meaningful bonds with them.

Parents with a dismissive-avoidant attachment style play a crucial role in shaping their children's attachment styles. Their behaviors, reflecting their preference for independence and emotional detachment within the parent-child relationship, may inadvertently prioritize their own needs and desires over those of their children. Viewing emotional intimacy and vulnerability as signs of weakness, these parents may struggle to provide the emotional support and validation that their children need, inadvertently fostering feelings of insecurity and emotional distance.

Children of parents with a dismissive-avoidant attachment style may internalize their parents' emotional unavailability, leading them to adopt similar coping mechanisms in their own relationships. They may learn to suppress their own emotions and avoid seeking support or closeness from others, fearing rejection or vulnerability. This can result in difficulties forming close, intimate relationships later in life, as they struggle to trust others and express their own emotions openly.

The dismissive-avoidant attachment style can create a dynamic within the parent-child relationship characterized by emotional distance and a lack of warmth or intimacy. Children may feel emotionally neglected or overlooked by their parents, leading to feelings of abandonment or rejection. Additionally, they may struggle to develop a secure sense of self and may experience challenges in forming healthy, fulfilling relationships with others.

While the dismissive-avoidant attachment style can pose significant challenges within the parent-child relationship, it's important to remember that change is possible. Both parties can work towards overcoming feelings of emotional detachment and a reluctance to engage in deep, meaningful connections. Recognizing and addressing these patterns can be crucial for fostering a more emotionally attuned and supportive parent-child dynamic characterized by mutual understanding, empathy, and closeness.

- **Fearful-avoidant attachment**

Individuals with a fearful-avoidant attachment style bring their conflicting desires for intimacy and independence into their parent-child relationships, shaping the dynamics and interactions between parent and child. In the parent-child dynamic, these individuals may experience an internal tug-of-war between their longing for closeness and fear of rejection or abandonment. As a result, children of parents with a fearful-avoidant attachment style may perceive their parents as unpredictable or inconsistent in their emotional availability, struggling to navigate the complexities of their relationship.

Parents with a fearful-avoidant attachment style may exhibit behaviors that reflect their internal conflict between intimacy and independence within the parent-child relationship. They may fluctuate between moments of closeness and emotional withdrawal, leaving their children feeling uncertain or insecure in their bond with them. These parents may inadvertently send mixed signals to their children, leading them to question the stability and reliability of their relationship.

Children of parents with a fearful-avoidant attachment style may internalize their parents' ambivalence toward emotional intimacy, leading them to develop their own fears and insecurities in relationships. They may crave emotional closeness and connection with their parents but fear getting hurt or rejected in the process. This can lead to difficulties trusting others and forming secure attachments later in life as they struggle to reconcile their desire for intimacy with their fear of vulnerability.

Within the parent-child relationship, the fearful-avoidant attachment style can create a dynamic characterized by unpredictability and emotional turbulence. Children may experience a profound sense of instability or insecurity in their relationship with their parents, never knowing when their parent will be emotionally available or distant. This can lead to intense feelings of anxiety or confusion as children grapple with their own desires for closeness and independence in the face of their parents' ambivalence.

Overall, the fearful-avoidant attachment style can pose significant challenges within the parent-child relationship as both parties navigate the complexities of intimacy and independence while grappling with their own fears and insecurities. It is crucial to recognize and address these patterns as soon as possible. Doing so can be essential for fostering a more stable and emotionally secure parent-child dynamic characterized by trust, understanding, and mutual support.

A study published in the Journal of Personality and Social Psychology found that individuals with secure attachment styles tended to experience less severe grief symptoms and greater emotional resilience in response to loss. In contrast, those with insecure attachment styles were more likely to experience heightened grief and emotional distress.

Understanding the influence of attachment styles on grief response can offer valuable insights into individuals' coping mechanisms and emotional reactions to anticipatory grief. By acknowledging the role of attachment in shaping individuals' grief responses, caregivers and loved ones can offer tailored support and interventions. This understanding equips them to help individuals navigate the complexities of anticipatory grief with compassion and resilience.

Why Understanding Your Attachment Style is Important

Each style influences how individuals perceive and respond to relationships, including those with aging parents and family members.

Impact of Attachment Styles on Anticipatory Grief:

- Secure Attachment:
  - Caregivers with secure attachment styles tend to offer consistent support and validation to their aging parents.
  - They approach anticipatory grief with openness, empathy, and a willingness to express emotions.
  - Securely attached families may experience greater cohesion and communication during the grieving process, fostering mutual support and understanding.

- Anxious-Preoccupied Attachment:
  - Caregivers with anxious-preoccupied attachment styles may struggle with heightened anxiety and fear of abandonment.
  - They may exhibit over-involvement or clinginess in caregiving roles, seeking constant reassurance from their aging parents.
  - Anticipatory grief may amplify feelings of uncertainty and distress, leading to difficulty in managing emotions and setting boundaries.

- Dismissive-Avoidant Attachment:
  - Caregivers with dismissive-avoidant attachment styles prioritize independence and self-reliance.
  - They may struggle to express emotions or seek support from others, preferring to cope with anticipatory grief internally.
  - Dismissive-avoidant individuals may downplay the significance of the impending loss, leading to a lack of emotional connection and support within the family.

- Fearful-Avoidant Attachment:
    - Caregivers with fearful-avoidant attachment styles experience conflicting desires for intimacy and independence.
    - They may grapple with trust issues and fear of rejection, which can complicate their ability to provide effective support to their aging parents.
    - Anticipatory grief may trigger feelings of vulnerability and anxiety, exacerbating challenges in navigating caregiving responsibilities and emotional expression.

Recognize Your Attachment Style: Caregivers and family members can empower themselves by engaging in introspection and understanding their own attachment styles. This self-awareness can be a powerful tool in navigating anticipatory grief.

Foster Open Communication: By creating a supportive environment for discussing emotions and concerns related to anticipatory grief, caregivers can foster a sense of understanding and support within the family. This can help them feel less alone in their journey.

Seek Professional Support: Therapy or counseling can offer caregivers and family members valuable insights and coping strategies for navigating anticipatory grief within the context of their attachment styles. This professional guidance can provide a sense of reassurance and help alleviate feelings of overwhelm.

Conclusion: Attachment theory provides a framework for understanding how caregivers and families navigate anticipatory grief. By recognizing the influence of attachment styles and fostering open communication and support, individuals can navigate this challenging journey with greater awareness, empathy, and resilience.

Cultural and Societal Perspectives: How Different Cultures Approach Aging and Grief

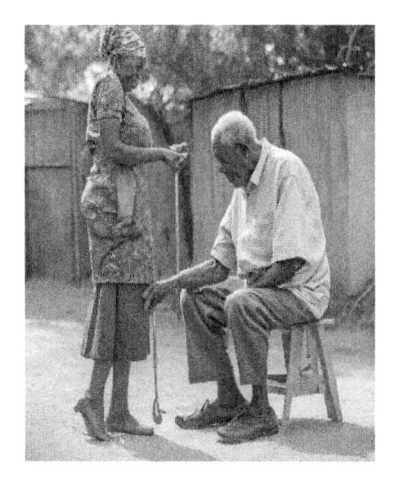

Examining Cultural Attitudes Toward Aging & Death

Cultural attitudes toward aging and death vary widely across different societies and can profoundly shape individuals' experiences of anticipatory grief. In some cultures, aging is revered as a natural and inevitable part of life, with older adults held in high esteem for their wisdom and life experience. In contrast, other cultures may view aging as a burden or a sign of weakness, leading to stigmatization and marginalization of older adults.

Studies have shown that cultural attitudes toward aging can significantly impact individuals' perceptions of aging and death. A cross-cultural study published in the International Journal of Aging and Human Development found that cultural values and beliefs about aging influenced individuals' attitudes toward aging and their expectations for later life. For example, cultures that prioritize interdependence and family cohesion may place a greater emphasis on caregiving and support for aging parents. In contrast, cultures that emphasize independence and self-reliance may place greater value on autonomy and personal responsibility in old age.

The Influence of Cultural Beliefs on Grief Expression

Cultural beliefs and traditions surrounding grief vary widely across different societies and cultures, each offering unique perspectives and practices for coping with loss. For example, in many Western cultures, such as the United States and parts of Europe, grief may be expressed more privately, with individuals encouraged to mourn in solitude or within the confines of their immediate family. While public displays of grief are not uncommon, there may be societal expectations to "move on" relatively quickly after a loss.

Conversely, in cultures like Mexico, India, and parts of Africa, communal mourning rituals are deeply ingrained in the fabric of society. These cultures often embrace elaborate funeral ceremonies, memorial services, and public displays of grief, allowing the community to unite to honor the deceased and support the grieving family. For instance, in Mexico, the Día de los Muertos (Day of the Dead) is a vibrant celebration where families gather to remember and honor their loved ones who have passed away, transforming grief into a colorful and joyful commemoration.

It's fascinating to note how cultural beliefs about the afterlife and spiritual continuity can profoundly shape our responses to grief. In cultures that hold beliefs in reincarnation or an afterlife, death is often viewed as a natural part of the eternal cycle of life. For example, in Hinduism, death is seen as a transition of the soul to another realm, where it continues its spiritual journey. This perspective provides comfort and solace to the bereaved, as they believe that their loved ones live on in some form beyond the physical realm.

Research supports the notion that cultural beliefs and practices significantly shape individuals' experiences of grief and their coping mechanisms. A study published in the Journal of Cross-Cultural Psychology found that individuals from collectivist cultures emphasizing community and interdependence tend to rely more on social support networks and communal grieving practices to cope with loss. In contrast, those from individualistic cultures, which prioritize personal autonomy and self-reliance, may prefer more private and reflective forms of grief expression.

Understanding and respecting the diversity of cultural attitudes toward aging, death, and grief is crucial in developing more inclusive and culturally sensitive approaches to supporting individuals and families facing anticipatory grief. It's important to honor the unique traditions and beliefs of diverse cultural communities while providing compassionate and culturally competent care to those navigating the complexities of loss and bereavement. This approach fosters empathy and understanding, allowing us to better support those in grief.

Challenges of Watching Parents Grow Older

Facing Mortality: Confronting the Inevitability of Loss

Processing the Reality of Parental Mortality

As parents age, adult children are inevitably confronted with the stark reality of parental mortality. The once-invincible figures of our childhood now face the same vulnerabilities and frailties as any other mortal being. This realization can be a profound and unsettling experience, challenging our perceptions of our parents as caregivers and protectors.

Studies have delved into the emotional impact of acknowledging parental mortality on adult children, shedding light on the complex array of responses that this realization can evoke. For instance, a study published in the Journal of Aging Studies explored the psychological ramifications of confronting parental mortality among adult children. The findings revealed that many adult children grapple with a myriad of emotions, ranging from profound sadness and grief to overwhelming anxiety and denial. This emotional tumult reflects the deep-seated attachment and dependence that adult children may still harbor toward their parents, making it difficult to reconcile the inevitability of their mortality.

Furthermore, the acknowledgment of parental mortality can disrupt established family dynamics and roles, triggering feelings of helplessness and vulnerability in adult children. The shift from viewing parents as strong and capable figures to recognizing their fragility and mortality can challenge long-held beliefs and assumptions about the parent-child relationship. Adult children may struggle to navigate this newfound vulnerability, grappling with feelings of uncertainty and insecurity as they confront the prospect of life without their parents.

Moreover, the study underscored the importance of open communication and support in helping adult children navigate the emotional terrain of parental mortality. By providing a safe space for expression and validation of their feelings, adult children can begin to process and come to terms with the inevitability of parental mortality. Additionally, access to resources such as therapy or support groups can offer valuable avenues for coping and resilience-building in the face of this existential challenge.

Overall, the acknowledgment of parental mortality represents a significant milestone in the adult-child-parent relationship, marking a transition from dependency to autonomy and confronting the existential realities of life and death. By acknowledging and exploring the emotional complexity of this experience, adult children can begin to navigate the journey of anticipatory grief with greater understanding, compassion, and resilience.

Coping with Existential Anxiety and Fear of Loss

Existential anxiety is a profound psychological phenomenon that arises from deep contemplation of existential questions about life, death, freedom, and the ultimate meaning of existence. Stemming from an individual's introspective examination of their place in the universe and their relationship to the larger cosmos, existential anxiety reflects the tension between the desire for meaning and the recognition of life's inherent uncertainties.

At its core, existential anxiety emerges when individuals confront the existential realities of human existence, including the inevitability of death, the limitations of human knowledge, and the search for purpose and significance in a vast and seemingly indifferent universe. This existential angst can be triggered by experiences such as losing a loved one, existential crises, or profound philosophical reflections on the nature of existence.

Existential anxiety is characterized by a deep sense of unease, disquiet, and existential dread as individuals grapple with the profound questions of existence. It can manifest as feelings of existential isolation, alienation, and a pervasive sense of meaninglessness or nihilism. Individuals experiencing existential anxiety may find themselves overwhelmed by existential questions, pondering the purpose of their lives and the meaning of their existence in the face of life's uncertainties.

Furthermore, existential anxiety often involves a heightened awareness of mortality and the transient nature of human existence. The contemplation of death and the finite nature of life can evoke profound feelings of fear, dread, and existential despair as individuals confront the inevitability of their own mortality and the impermanence of all things.

A study published in the Journal of Psychosocial Nursing and Mental Health Services delved into the experiences of caregivers of older adults, revealing prevalent existential concerns among this demographic. The study found that caregivers often grappled with profound existential questions related to the aging process, mortality, and future uncertainties. These existential concerns were associated with heightened levels of psychological distress, including symptoms of depression and anxiety.

Furthermore, the study highlighted the need for targeted support and interventions to address the existential fears and anxieties experienced by caregivers of older adults. Existential therapy, which focuses on exploring and resolving existential concerns, may offer valuable tools and techniques for caregivers to cope with their existential distress. Additionally, providing caregivers with opportunities for existential reflection and meaning making can help them find greater purpose and resilience in their caregiving roles.

Moreover, statistics underscore the prevalence and significance of existential anxiety among caregivers of older adults. According to the National Alliance for Caregiving, approximately 61% of caregivers report experiencing significant emotional stress, with existential concerns often contributing to this distress. Furthermore, studies have shown that caregivers experiencing high levels of existential anxiety are at increased risk of burnout, compassion fatigue, and compromised mental health.

In light of these findings, it is essential to recognize and address the existential concerns of older adult caregivers as part of comprehensive support and intervention efforts. By acknowledging and validating caregivers' existential fears and providing them with the necessary resources and support, healthcare professionals can help mitigate psychological distress and enhance the well-being of both caregivers and the older adults under their care.

Role Reversal: Navigating Changes in Parent-Child Dynamics

Shifting from Dependence to Independence

As parents age, adult children often find themselves navigating a gradual shift in parent-child dynamics as the roles of caregiver and dependent begin to blur. The once-dependable authority figures may now rely on their children for support and assistance with daily tasks, reversing the traditional roles of dependence and care.

Studies examining the dynamic of role reversal between aging parents and adult children have revealed the intricate emotional landscape that accompanies this transition. One such study, published in the Journal of Aging Studies, delved into the lived experiences of adult children navigating the complexities of assuming caregiving responsibilities for their aging parents. The findings shed light on the profound emotional challenges inherent in this role reversal process.

The study illuminated how adult children often find themselves grappling with a myriad of conflicting emotions as they transition from the role of the cared-for to that of the caregiver. For many adult children, assuming caregiving responsibilities for their aging parents represents a significant departure from their previous roles as sons or daughters, challenging deeply ingrained familial dynamics and expectations.

The findings of the study highlighted that adult children commonly experience feelings of guilt, as they struggle to reconcile their desire to provide adequate care and support for their parents with the demands of their own lives and responsibilities. The inherent tension between caregiving duties and personal aspirations can evoke profound feelings of ambivalence and conflict, as adult children navigate the delicate balance between meeting their parents' needs and maintaining their own autonomy and well-being.

Furthermore, the study revealed that adult children may also grapple with feelings of resentment, as they confront the emotional and logistical challenges associated with caregiving. Balancing caregiving responsibilities with work, family, and personal commitments can take a toll on adult children's physical and emotional well-being, leading to feelings of frustration, exhaustion, and resentment towards their parents or the situation at hand.

Overall, the study underscored the complex interplay of emotions that characterize the role reversal dynamic between aging parents and adult children. By shedding light on the emotional challenges faced by both parties, the findings of the study underscore the importance of providing support and resources to help families navigate this transition with compassion, empathy, and resilience.

Balancing Autonomy with Caregiving Responsibilities

As adult children transition into caregiving roles for their aging parents, they face the delicate task of preserving their parents' autonomy while fulfilling their caregiving duties. This delicate balance requires a nuanced approach that prioritizes empathy, effective communication, and respect for the aging individual's inherent dignity.

Studies exploring the relationship between autonomy and well-being among older adults have underscored the importance of maintaining independence and control over one's life. One such study, published in the Journal of Gerontological Nursing, delved into the impact of autonomy on the overall well-being and quality of life of older adults. The findings revealed that older adults who retained a sense of control and autonomy reported higher levels of life satisfaction and psychological well-being than those who experienced a loss of independence.

The study underscored the manifold advantages of autonomy for older adults, including a sense of empowerment, self-efficacy, and personal fulfillment. Upholding autonomy enables older adults to make choices that reflect their preferences, values, and aspirations, fostering a sense of control and self-determination in their daily lives.

Moreover, the study accentuated the role autonomy plays in bolstering older adults' physical and emotional health. By retaining control over aspects of their lives, such as daily routines, social interactions, and healthcare decisions, older adults can experience increased autonomy and a sense of mastery over their environment, enhancing their overall well-being and quality of life.

In caregiving, supporting older adults' autonomy involves:

- Actively involving them in decision-making processes.
- Respecting their preferences and choices.
- Providing opportunities for self-expression and independence whenever possible.

By recognizing and upholding the importance of autonomy in caregiving relationships, adult children can foster a sense of dignity, respect, and empowerment in their aging parents, ultimately enhancing their overall well-being and quality of life.

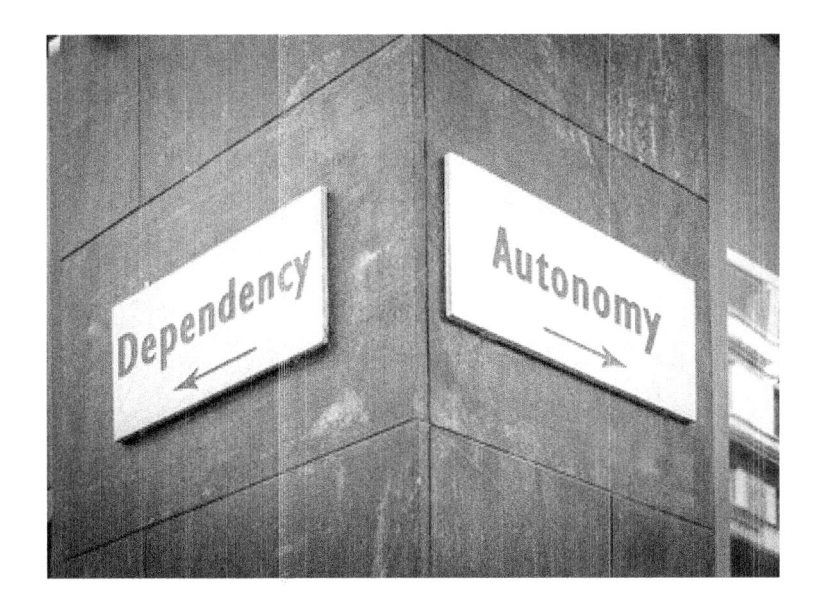

Coping with Uncertainty:
Balancing Hope and Realism
Managing Ambiguous Loss and Grief Limbo

As parents age and confront declining health, adult children are frequently thrust into the realm of ambiguous loss and the emotional limbo of anticipatory grief.

Ambiguous loss refers to a type of loss that lacks clear resolution or closure, leaving individuals in a perpetual state of uncertainty and emotional upheaval. In the context of caregiving for aging parents, this ambiguity arises from the gradual decline in health and functioning, coupled with the looming specter of eventual loss.

Grief limbo, on the other hand, encapsulates the experience of being caught between the anticipation of loss and the absence of closure. It is a state of emotional liminality characterized by fluctuating emotions, conflicting desires, and an overarching sense of disorientation. In this state, caregivers may oscillate between hope and despair, acceptance and denial, as they grapple with the profound uncertainties of the future.

Research has shed light on the unique challenges posed by managing ambiguous loss and grief limbo in the context of caregiving for aging parents. A study published in the Journal of Loss and Trauma delved into the experiences of caregivers of older adults, revealing the heightened levels of stress and emotional distress they often endure. Caregivers navigating anticipatory grief are confronted with the paradox of mourning a loss that has not yet occurred, leading to a complex interplay of emotions and psychological turmoil.

The study underscored the need for targeted interventions and support mechanisms to assist caregivers in navigating the complexities of ambiguous loss and grief limbo. By providing caregivers with resources, education, and coping strategies tailored to the unique challenges of anticipatory grief, healthcare professionals and support networks can help alleviate the emotional burden and enhance caregivers' resilience in the face of uncertainty.

Mindfulness and Acceptance in the Face of Uncertainty

MINDFULNESS

Cultivating mindfulness and acceptance can serve as invaluable coping mechanisms for individuals navigating the turbulent waters of anticipatory grief amidst uncertainty. Mindfulness, in essence, involves purposefully paying attention to the present moment without judgment.

BE HERE NOW

It encompasses practices such as meditation, deep breathing exercises, and guided imagery, all of which aim to foster a heightened awareness of one's thoughts, feelings, and bodily sensations.

Mindfulness techniques can offer individuals a much-needed respite from the relentless barrage of worries and fears about the future, providing a safe harbor in the storm of anticipatory grief. By embracing the present moment with acceptance and non-judgment, individuals can cultivate a sense of calm and stability, offering a glimmer of hope amidst the turmoil.

Research has illuminated the transformative power of mindfulness-based interventions in mitigating the psychological distress associated with anticipatory grief. A comprehensive meta-analysis published in the Journal of Consulting and Clinical Psychology synthesized findings from numerous studies. It concluded that mindfulness-based interventions yielded significant reductions in symptoms of anxiety and depression across diverse populations, including caregivers of older adults.

These interventions equip individuals with practical tools to navigate the complex terrain of anticipatory grief, empowering them to take control and cultivate resilience and emotional well-being in the face of uncertainty. By integrating mindfulness practices into their daily routines, individuals can foster a deeper sense of self-awareness, acceptance, and inner peace, thereby enhancing their capacity to cope with the challenges of caregiving and anticipatory grief.

Managing Caregiver Stress: Addressing the Emotional Toll of Caregiving

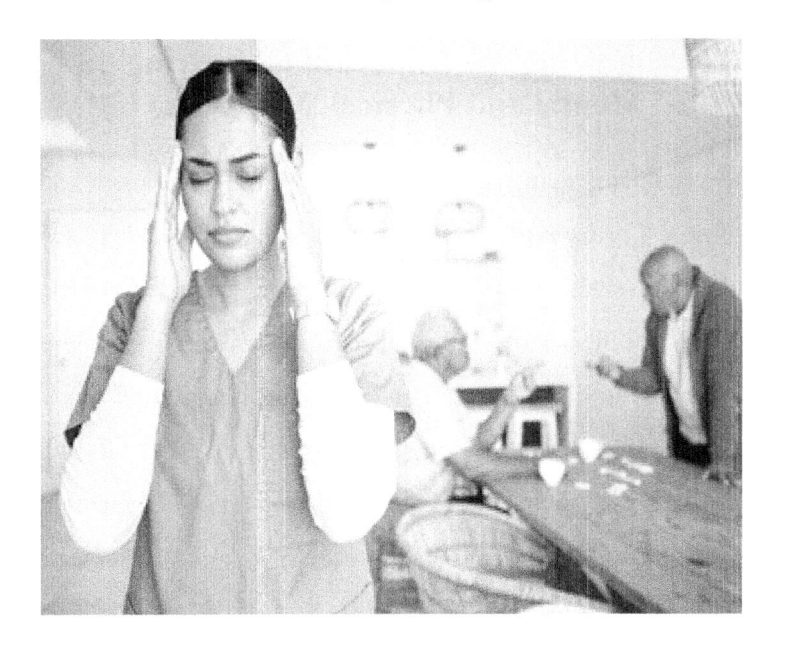

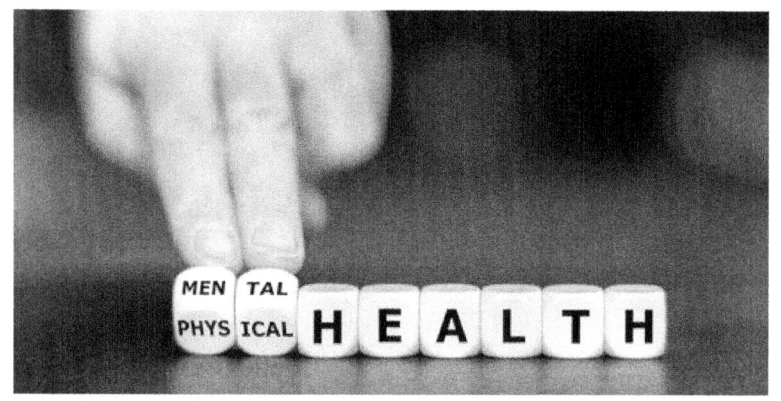

Recognizing the Impact of Caregiving on Mental and Physical Well-Being

The role of caregiving is laden with emotional complexities and challenges, often exacting a substantial toll on individuals who find themselves at the intersection of caregiving duties, personal obligations, and professional responsibilities. Numerous studies have underscored the heightened risk of stress, depression, and burnout among caregivers of older adults, shedding light on the profound impact of caregiving on caregivers' mental and physical well-being.

Research has unveiled the profound impact of caregiver stress on both mental and physical health, shedding light on the myriad health issues faced by those who take on caregiving responsibilities. Psychological disorders such as depression and anxiety are prevalent among caregivers, with studies indicating a notable disparity in mental health outcomes compared to non-caregivers. For instance, a study published in the Journal of the American Geriatrics Society reported that caregivers of older adults are at a significantly higher risk of experiencing depression and anxiety than their non-caregiving counterparts. The research findings revealed that a staggering percentage of caregivers, upwards of 40% in some studies, grapple with symptoms of depression, highlighting the pervasive nature of mental health challenges within this population. Moreover, anxiety disorders affect a considerable portion of caregivers, with prevalence rates exceeding 30% in certain studies. These statistics underscore the urgent need for targeted interventions and support systems to safeguard caregivers' mental health and well-being, ensuring they receive the assistance and resources necessary to navigate the demands of caregiving while preserving their own health and quality of life.

The findings of such studies emphasize the critical importance of recognizing and addressing the multifaceted needs of caregivers, who play a pivotal role in supporting and caring for aging parents or loved ones. By implementing comprehensive support programs and interventions tailored to caregivers' unique challenges and stressors, healthcare providers and policymakers can mitigate caregiver stress's adverse effects, thereby promoting caregivers' health and resilience and enhancing the quality of care provided to older adults.

Implementing Self-Care Strategies for Caregivers

In the realm of caregiving for aging parents, prioritizing self-care emerges as not just a personal indulgence but an essential practice vital for both the caregiver's well-being and the quality of care provided. Research across various disciplines resoundingly underscores the pivotal role of self-care strategies in mitigating the detrimental effects of caregiver stress and burnout. Studies reveal that caregivers who actively engage in self-care report lower stress levels and enhanced psychological well-being, thereby enhancing their capacity to provide effective and compassionate care to their loved ones.

Consider a study published in the Journal of Aging and Health, which delved into the impact of physical activity on caregiver stress. Findings indicated that caregivers who integrated regular exercise into their routines experienced significantly reduced stress levels and reported greater overall psychological health than their sedentary counterparts. These insights highlight the profound benefits that seemingly simple lifestyle modifications, like engaging in physical activity, can yield for caregivers' mental and emotional resilience.

Furthermore, research elucidates how self-care practices extend beyond mere stress reduction, encompassing a spectrum of benefits that resonate across various dimensions of caregivers' lives. Studies have shown that caregivers who prioritize self-care experience improved emotional well-being, enhanced cognitive functioning, and greater resilience in the face of adversity. Moreover, engaging in self-care activities fosters a sense of empowerment and autonomy, enabling caregivers to maintain a semblance of control amidst the unpredictable challenges of caregiving.

As such, the implementation of self-care strategies emerges not merely as a luxury but as an imperative for caregivers navigating the intricate landscape of caring for aging parents. By embracing self-care practices, caregivers fortify their own well-being and optimize their capacity to provide compassionate and effective care to their loved ones. This chapter endeavors to illuminate evidence-based self-care strategies tailored to address the multifaceted demands of caregiving, empowering caregivers to navigate their caregiving journey with resilience, grace, and an unwavering commitment to their own well-being, thereby showcasing their strength and capability.

Mindfulness-Based Stress Reduction (MBSR)

Caring for aging parents can be emotionally and physically demanding, often leading to increased stress and burnout among caregivers. In the midst of these challenges, finding ways to manage stress and promote well-being becomes essential. One approach that has gained significant attention for its effectiveness in reducing stress is Mindfulness-Based Stress Reduction (MBSR), offering a beacon of hope and relief for caregivers.

What is MBSR?

MBSR is an evidence-based program developed by Dr. Jon Kabat-Zinn in the late 1970s at the University of Massachusetts Medical Center. It combines mindfulness meditation, body awareness, and yoga, providing practical tools for caregivers to cultivate greater awareness of the present moment and develop coping strategies for managing stress.

As caregivers navigate the challenges of providing care for aging parents, incorporating mindfulness practices into their daily routine can offer invaluable support in managing stress and promoting well-being.

Let's delve deeper into each of these mindful practices:

Mindful Breathing: Mindful breathing is a simple yet powerful technique that can offer profound benefits for caregivers amidst the demands of their responsibilities.

- **Grounding Anchor in Busyness:** Amidst the whirlwind of caregiving tasks and responsibilities, finding moments of stillness and presence can be challenging yet essential for maintaining well-being. Mindful breathing serves as a grounding anchor, allowing caregivers to pause, reconnect with themselves, and find a sense of calm amidst the chaos. By carving out a few moments each day to practice mindful breathing, caregivers create a sanctuary of tranquility within their hectic lives.

- **Creating a Quiet Space:** The environment plays a crucial role in the practice of mindful breathing. Caregivers can designate a specific spot in their home, a cozy corner, a tranquil garden, or a comfortable chair by a window, where they can retreat for a few moments of peace and solitude. This quiet space, a tangible refuge, serves as a practical setting for mindfulness practice. By removing oneself from the hustle and bustle of daily life and immersing oneself in this environment, caregivers can experience a deeper level of mindfulness.

- **Heightened Awareness of Breath:** As caregivers settle into their quiet space, they can begin the practice of mindful breathing by focusing their attention on the breath. With eyes closed if comfortable, caregivers tune into the sensations of each inhale and exhale, observing the gentle rhythm of their breath. They may notice the expansion and contraction of their chest or abdomen with each breath, anchoring their awareness in the present moment. This immediate awareness of breath serves as a focal point for mindfulness practice, providing instant relief and calm.

- **Immersion in the Present Moment:** The essence of mindful breathing lies in fully immersing oneself in the present moment, letting go of past regrets and future worries. As caregivers concentrate on their breath, they release the grip of distractions and concerns that often weigh heavily on their minds. Instead, they embrace the here and now, finding solace in the simplicity of each inhalation and exhalation. This profound immersion in the present moment cultivates a sense of peace and serenity amidst life's complexities, a practice that can truly empower caregivers.

Benefits of Mindful Breathing for Caregivers: Numerous studies have highlighted the benefits of mindful breathing for caregivers' well-being:

- **Stress Reduction:** Mindful breathing has been shown to reduce stress levels by activating the body's relaxation response, lowering cortisol levels, and promoting a sense of calm.
- **Emotional Regulation:** Regular mindful breathing enhances emotional regulation skills, allowing caregivers to navigate challenging emotions with greater ease and resilience.
- **Improved Focus and Clarity:** By training the mind to focus on the breath, caregivers experience improved concentration and mental clarity, enhancing their ability to attend to caregiving tasks with presence and efficiency.

➢ **Enhanced Self-Care:** Mindful breathing is a cornerstone of self-care. It offers caregivers a simple yet effective tool for recharging and replenishing their energy reserves.

Incorporating mindful breathing into their daily routine empowers caregivers, giving them a sense of control and capability, to navigate the ups and downs of caregiving with greater ease, resilience, and well-being.

Body Scan Meditation: This is not just any meditation, it's a powerful technique for cultivating body awareness and releasing tension held within the body. Body scan meditation is a potent technique for enhancing body awareness, relieving tension, and promoting relaxation.

- **Setting Aside Dedicated Time:** Caregivers should carve out dedicated time in their daily schedule to reap the full benefits of body scan meditation. Consistent practice is vital, whether at the beginning of the day to set a positive tone or at the end to unwind and release accumulated stress. By prioritizing this time for self-care, caregivers honor their physical and emotional well-being.

- **Creating a Comfortable Environment:** Find a quiet and comfortable space to lie down without distractions. Create a soothing ambiance with soft lighting, gentle music, or nature sounds, if desired. Dim the lights, silence your phone, and make yourself cozy with blankets or pillows to support your body during the practice.

- **Engaging in Systematic Attention:** As you settle into your chosen position, close your eyes and bring your attention inward. Begin the body scan by systematically directing your focus to different parts of your body, starting from your toes and slowly moving upward to your head. Pay attention to each body part individually, noticing any sensations, tensions, or areas of discomfort without judgment or resistance.

- **Cultivating Nonjudgmental Awareness:** The heart of body scan meditation lies in cultivating nonjudgmental awareness of bodily sensations. As you scan each body part, it's essential to refrain from labeling sensations as 'good' or 'bad.' Instead, adopt an attitude of curiosity and acceptance, allowing sensations to arise and pass without attachment. This practice is a powerful tool that encourages caregivers to be more compassionate towards themselves, fostering a sense of acceptance and understanding. It's about acknowledging the body's needs without judgment, which is a crucial aspect of self-care.

Benefits of Body Scan Meditation for Caregivers: Body scan meditation offers a plethora of benefits for caregivers' physical and emotional well-being:

➢ **Stress Reduction:** By systematically relaxing each body part, body scan meditation activates the body's relaxation response, reducing stress hormones and promoting a state of calm.

➢ **Tension Release:** As caregivers tune into bodily sensations, they become aware of tension or discomfort in the body. They can release accumulated tension through gentle attention and breath awareness and promote muscular relaxation.

➢ **Enhanced Body Awareness:** Regular practice of body scan meditation not only heightens body awareness but also empowers caregivers to detect subtle changes or signals of stress or fatigue early on. This heightened awareness is a powerful tool, enabling caregivers to prioritize self-care and proactively address their body's needs. It's like having an early warning system for their well-being. This aspect of the practice can instill a sense of security and confidence in caregivers, knowing that they are equipped to respond to their body's signals effectively.

Incorporating body scan meditation into their self-care regimen not only provides a tool for caregivers to honor their body's needs and release tension but also empowers them to foster relaxation amidst the demanding nature of caregiving. This practice puts the control back in their hands, allowing them to manage their stress more effectively. By taking this proactive step, caregivers are equipping themselves with a powerful tool to navigate the challenges of their role with resilience and strength.

Mindful Movement: Incorporating mindful movement into your daily routine is a powerful way to nurture both body and mind amidst the challenges of caregiving. Caregivers can embrace activities like walking meditation or gentle yoga and the numerous benefits they offer:

- **Reconnecting with Your Body:** Caregiving often involves putting the needs of others before your own, leading to a disconnect from your body's signals and sensations. Mindful movement provides an opportunity to reestablish this connection by tuning into your body's physical sensations and movements. Whether it's the sensation of your feet touching the ground during walking meditation or the gentle stretch of your muscles in yoga, each movement serves as a reminder of your embodied presence.

- **Cultivating Presence and Awareness:** Engaging in mindful movement offers an immediate respite from the stress and worries of caregiving. As you walk mindfully or practice yoga, focus your attention on your body's sensations, movements, and rhythms. This shift in focus can provide a much-needed break, offering a sense of peace and clarity in the present moment. It's like a breath of fresh air in the midst of a busy day, instantly relieving the tension and allowing you to recharge.

- **Enhancing Stress Reduction and Relaxation:** Mindful movement is not just a tool, but a powerful instrument for caregivers to take control of their stress levels and find relaxation. The deliberate, gentle movements of walking meditation or yoga can be a soothing balm on aching muscles, triggering relaxation responses in the body, reducing cortisol levels and promoting a sense of ease. Through mindful movement, caregivers can create a sanctuary of tranquility amidst the demands of caregiving, replenishing their energy and resilience, and feeling empowered in their self-care journey.

Nurturing Self-Care and Well-being: Prioritizing mindful movement as part of your self-care routine is not just an act, but a testament of self-compassion and nurturing. Caregivers honor their well-being and resilience by carving out time for activities that nourish their body and mind. The mindful movement offers a space for caregivers to replenish their inner resources, fostering a sense of vitality and balance amidst the demands of caregiving, and making them feel more valued and cared for.

➢ **Fostering Mind-Body Integration:** Mindful movement promotes harmonious integration of mind and body, fostering a deep sense of connection and wholeness. As caregivers synchronize their movements with their breath and cultivate awareness of bodily sensations, they facilitate a profound union of mind, body, and spirit. This integration supports holistic well-being and resilience, empowering caregivers to navigate the complexities of caregiving with grace and presence.

Incorporating mindful movement into your daily routine offers a sanctuary of peace and rejuvenation amidst the demands of caregiving. Whether a mindful walk in nature or a gentle yoga practice, these activities provide caregivers with a sacred space to nurture body, mind, and soul, fostering resilience and well-being.

Mindful Eating: Mindful eating is not just about what you eat; it's about how you eat and the awareness you bring to the experience. Let's delve into the benefits of incorporating mindfulness into your eating habits:

- **Heightened Sensory Awareness:** The process of mindful eating encourages you to engage all your senses in the eating experience. By paying attention to your food's colors, textures, and aromas, you become more attuned to the sensory pleasures of eating. This heightened sensory awareness enhances your enjoyment of food and deepens your connection to the present moment.

- **Improved Digestion:** Mindful eating isn't just a philosophical concept; it has practical benefits too. Chewing slowly and mindfully allows your body to better digest and absorb nutrients from your food. Taking the time to chew each bite thoroughly aids in the breakdown of food particles, making it easier for your digestive system to process. This can help prevent digestive issues such as bloating, indigestion, and discomfort.

- **Enhanced Satisfaction and Fulfillment:** Mindful eating is like a secret ingredient that can enhance your eating experience. It encourages you to savor each bite and fully appreciate the flavors and textures of your food. By eating slowly and mindfully, you may find that you feel more satisfied and fulfilled with smaller portions. This can help prevent overeating and promote a healthier relationship with food.

- **Increased Gratitude and Appreciation:** Cultivating gratitude for your food's nourishment is a central aspect of mindful eating. By recognizing the effort and resources that went into producing your meal, you develop a greater appreciation for the interconnectedness of food and well-being. This sense of gratitude can enhance your eating experience and foster a deeper connection to the food you consume.

- **One of the most powerful aspects of** mindful eating is its ability to support emotional regulation. By tuning into your body's hunger and fullness cues, you become more attuned to your physical and emotional needs. This practice can help you develop a greater awareness of emotional eating triggers and habits, providing a supportive framework for making more conscious choices about what, when, and how much you eat. This, in turn, can lead to improved emotional regulation and overall well-being, making you feel more in control of your eating habits.

- **Mind-Body Connection:** Mindful eating fosters a deeper connection between your mind and body, promoting holistic well-being. By approaching meals with awareness and intention, you honor your body's nutritional needs and cultivate a sense of self-care and nourishment. This mind-body connection supports overall health and vitality, helping you physically and mentally thrive.

Incorporating mindful eating practices into your daily routine can be a transformative journey, revolutionizing your relationship with food and nourishing your body, mind, and soul. By savoring each bite with awareness and appreciation, you cultivate a more profound sense of gratitude, satisfaction, and well-being in your eating experience.

Mindful Communication: Engaging in the process of mindful communication with your loved ones and fellow caregivers is a powerful tool for fostering deeper connections and understanding. It's not just about talking; it's about genuinely connecting. This practice can make you and the person you're communicating with feel more heard, understood, and supported. Practice active listening by giving your full attention to the speaker without judgment or interruption. Listen not only to the words being spoken but also to the underlying emotions and concerns. Respond with compassion and empathy, validating the other person's experiences and emotions. By practicing mindful communication, you can create a supportive and nurturing environment for open dialogue and connection.

By incorporating these mindful practices into your daily life as a caregiver, you are not only taking care of your loved ones but also prioritizing your own well-being. This act of self-care is not selfish, but a necessary step in cultivating greater resilience, reducing stress, and enhancing your overall well-being. Remember to approach these practices with curiosity and kindness, allowing yourself the space to explore and grow on your journey of caregiving.

Communicating and Connecting Through Aging and Grief

Opening the Dialogue:

Breaking the Silence Surrounding Aging and Grief

Overcoming Taboos and Stigmas Around Death and Aging

In contemporary societies, conversations revolving around aging, death, and grief are often cloaked in discomfort and evaded due to prevailing taboos and stigmas. However, piercing through this veil of silence becomes imperative as research underscores the profound benefits of open communication in navigating the complexities of aging and end-of-life care. According to a study published in the Journal of the American Geriatrics Society, older adults who discuss their end-of-life wishes are substantially more likely to receive care that aligns with their preferences and values. Statistics reveal a significant correlation between open communication about end-of-life wishes and the satisfaction of care received by aging parents. The study indicated that nearly 80% of older adults who discussed their end-of-life preferences reported higher levels of satisfaction with their care than those who had not engaged in such conversations. These findings illuminate the transformative power of open communication in fostering a supportive environment where aging parents and their adult children can navigate the intricate terrain of aging and end-of-life care with clarity, dignity, and mutual understanding. By confronting taboos and stigmas head-on, individuals can pave the way for meaningful conversations that honor the wishes and values of aging parents while nurturing deeper connections and emotional well-being within the family unit.

Creating Safe Spaces for Honest and Conversations

Creating safe spaces for honest and vulnerable conversations between caregivers and aging parents is a multifaceted process that requires sensitivity, empathy, and active engagement. One crucial aspect of establishing such spaces is cultivating nonjudgmental attitudes and behaviors, where both parties feel free to express themselves without fear of criticism or condemnation. This can be achieved by practicing empathetic listening, wherein caregivers and aging parents strive to understand each other's perspectives and emotions without interruption or judgment.

Moreover, validating each other's experiences and emotions is paramount in creating safe spaces for communication. Caregivers can validate the feelings and concerns of aging parents by acknowledging their emotions and offering empathetic responses, fostering a sense of understanding and acceptance. Similarly, aging parents can validate the challenges and efforts of caregivers by expressing gratitude and appreciation for their support and dedication.

In addition to verbal communication, non-verbal cues such as eye contact, facial expressions, and body language are powerful tools in creating safe spaces for honest conversations. Maintaining open body language and eye contact not only conveys attentiveness and receptivity but also signals to the other party that their thoughts and feelings are valued and respected, thereby enhancing understanding and respect in the conversation.

Furthermore, the allocation of dedicated time and space for these conversations is a crucial step that can significantly enhance their effectiveness and impact. By scheduling regular check-ins or designated 'talk times', caregivers and aging parents can create an environment where they can openly discuss concerns, preferences, and feelings in a supportive and non-interruptive manner, thereby promoting emotional well-being and strengthening their bond.

By implementing these strategies and fostering an atmosphere of trust, empathy, and mutual respect, caregivers and aging parents can create safe spaces for honest and vulnerable conversations. These honest conversations facilitate open communication about aging and grief, strengthen their bond, and promote emotional well-being for both parties involved.

Strategies for Discussing Aging and End-of-Life Wishes

Initiating conversations about end-of-life wishes, a crucial role often taken on by caregivers, requires careful consideration and preparation to ensure that the dialogue is productive, respectful, and supportive. Here are some strategies for facilitating meaningful discussions:

- **Choosing an appropriate time and place:** Selecting the right time and setting for the conversation is crucial for fostering openness and comfort. Opt for a quiet, private space where both parties can speak freely without interruptions or distractions. Consider choosing a time when everyone involved is relaxed and receptive, avoiding moments of stress or tension.

- **Framing the conversation with empathy and compassion:** Approach the conversation with empathy and compassion, acknowledging the sensitivity and significance of the topic at hand. Express genuine concern and care for the aging parent's well-being, emphasizing that the purpose of the discussion is to ensure their wishes are honored and respected.

- **Actively listening to each other's concerns and desires:** Practice active listening by giving your full attention to the aging parent's thoughts, feelings, and preferences. Encourage them to express their concerns, desires, and fears openly and without judgment. Reflect on what you hear to ensure mutual understanding and validation of their perspective.

- **Open-ended questions and exploration:** Encourage open-ended questions and exploration to delve deeper into the aging parent's values, beliefs, and priorities regarding end-of-life care. Allow them the space to express their wishes comprehensively, covering topics such as medical interventions, quality of life preferences, and spiritual or cultural considerations.

- **Respecting autonomy and agency:** Honor the aging parent's autonomy and agency throughout the conversation, recognizing their right to make decisions about their own care and treatment. Avoid imposing personal beliefs or preferences onto them and empower them to assert their wishes confidently.

- **Documenting the conversation:** Consider documenting the outcomes of the conversation, such as advance directives or living wills, to ensure that the aging parent's wishes are formally recorded and communicated to relevant parties. Additionally, schedule regular check-ins to revisit and reassess their preferences, allowing for adjustments as circumstances evolve.

By implementing these strategies and fostering a supportive and respectful atmosphere, individuals can facilitate open and honest conversations about end-of-life wishes. These discussions, when approached with empathy and understanding, not only provide clarity and guidance for decision-making but also have the potential to bring families closer together, fostering a sense of unity and shared responsibility. They ensure that their loved one's preferences are understood and honored, promoting peace of mind and dignity for all involved.

Addressing Practical Matters

In addition to discussing end-of-life wishes, addressing practical matters such as advance directives and estate planning is crucial for ensuring that individuals' preferences are respected and their affairs are managed according to their wishes. Advance directives, which encompass documents like living wills and durable power of attorney for healthcare, empower individuals to outline their medical treatment preferences and designate a trusted individual to make healthcare decisions on their behalf if they cannot do so themselves.

Studies have demonstrated the importance of advance directives in facilitating care that aligns with individuals' values and preferences. According to research published in the Journal of the American Geriatrics Society, individuals with advance directives are more likely to receive care that reflects their end-of-life wishes, leading to higher rates of satisfaction with care and reduced emotional distress among both patients and their families. Moreover, advance care planning has been associated with positive outcomes such as decreased utilization of aggressive medical interventions near the end of life, resulting in improved quality of life and even decreased healthcare costs, offering a hopeful and optimistic perspective on the future.

Estate planning is another critical aspect of preparing for the future, allowing individuals to specify how their assets and possessions should be distributed after their death. According to a study published in the

Journal of Financial Planning, only a minority of adults have completed essential estate planning documents, such as wills or trusts, despite the significant impact these documents can have on asset distribution and resolving disputes among family members. By engaging in estate planning, individuals can provide clarity and peace of mind for themselves and their loved ones, ensuring their wishes are honored, and their affairs are managed according to their intentions.

Strengthening Bonds:

Finding Meaningful Ways to Connect with Aging Parents

Nurturing Emotional Connection Through Shared Activities

Finding meaningful ways to connect with aging parents is a source of joy and a vital component of maintaining strong family bonds and fostering emotional well-being. Whether it's sharing a meal, taking a leisurely walk, or pursuing shared interests and hobbies, these activities offer opportunities for quality time and intimate conversations that can deepen the relationship.

Scientific research underscores the importance of fostering emotional connections with aging parents for both parties. A study published in the Journal of Marriage and Family found that older adults who felt emotionally close to their adult children reported higher levels of life satisfaction and psychological well-being. Similarly, adult children who maintain strong emotional bonds with their aging parents are more likely to experience greater fulfillment in their own lives and relationships.

By prioritizing quality time and engaging in activities that promote emotional closeness, individuals can create meaningful connections with their aging parents that contribute to their overall well-being. These moments of connection strengthen family bonds and create cherished memories that endure beyond the challenges of aging and provide comfort and solace in times of need. Ultimately, investing in these relationships enriches the lives of aging parents and their adult children, fostering a sense of belonging, love, and support that transcends generations.

Seeking Support: Resources for Individuals and Families Facing Anticipatory Grief

Navigating anticipatory grief can indeed be emotionally taxing, and seeking professional support through therapy and counseling can offer invaluable assistance in coping with the complexities of caregiving and the emotional turmoil that accompanies anticipatory grief. These therapeutic interventions provide a safe and confidential space for individuals to process their feelings, explore their experiences, and develop effective coping strategies.

Therapy and counseling offer a range of benefits, including the opportunity to gain insight into one's emotions and behaviors, develop healthier coping mechanisms, and receive personalized guidance and support from trained professionals. By engaging in therapy, individuals can learn to navigate the unique challenges of anticipatory grief with resilience and self-compassion.

Accessing therapy and counseling services can be facilitated through various channels, including:

- **Individual therapy** involves one-on-one sessions with a licensed therapist or counselor specializing in grief, aging, or caregiving issues. These sessions provide a personalized approach tailored to the individual's needs and concerns.
- **Support Groups**: Don't face your challenges alone. Joining a support group for caregivers or individuals facing anticipatory grief can offer a powerful sense of community, validation, and understanding. These groups provide a platform for sharing experiences, receiving peer support, and learning from others who are going through similar challenges, making you feel less alone in your journey.
- **Online Counseling Platforms**: In today's digital age, many online platforms offer virtual counseling services. This innovative approach allows individuals to access therapy from the comfort and convenience of their own homes, eliminating the need for travel and providing flexible options for receiving support.
- **Community Mental Health Centers**: Community-based mental health centers often offer counseling services at reduced or sliding-scale fees based on income. These centers may provide a range of therapeutic modalities and support groups tailored to the community's needs.

- **Employee Assistance Programs (EAPs)**: Many workplaces provide Employee Assistance Programs (EAPs) that offer free or discounted counseling services to employees and their families. These programs provide confidential counseling sessions in-person or virtually, helping individuals deal with personal and work-related challenges.

Therapy and counseling are effective tools in mitigating symptoms of depression, anxiety, and grief in individuals facing anticipatory grief. A study published in the journal Psychotherapy Research revealed that participants who engaged in therapy reported significant improvements in their psychological well-being and overall quality of life. By accessing professional support, you can navigate anticipatory grief with greater resilience, self-awareness, and emotional well-being, instilling a sense of hope and optimism in your journey.

Peer Support Groups and Online Communities

Peer support groups are more than just gatherings of individuals who share common experiences, challenges, or circumstances. They are communities that come together to provide mutual support, encouragement, and understanding. In the context of anticipatory grief, these communities bring together individuals and families facing similar challenges related to aging, caregiving, and impending loss. They provide a safe and non-judgmental space for members to share their emotions, thoughts, and experiences, knowing they are among peers who can relate to their journey. Confidentiality is a key aspect of these groups, ensuring that what is shared within the group stays within the group.

Peer support groups typically operate under the guidance of trained facilitators or volunteers. These individuals, often with professional backgrounds in counseling or social work, ensure that meetings are structured, respectful, and conducive to open communication. They facilitate discussion, maintain a safe and supportive environment, and provide resources or referrals when needed. Meetings may take various formats, including in-person gatherings, virtual meetings, or online forums, allowing individuals to connect with peers regardless of geographical location or mobility constraints.

In peer support groups, members not only share their experiences and listen to others' stories, but they also gain practical advice and coping strategies. This exchange of empathy, validation, and emotional support not only provides comfort but also empowers members to navigate their journey through anticipatory grief with confidence. It offers insights, perspectives, and a sense of belonging that can help alleviate

142

feelings of isolation and loneliness often associated with this stage.

Peer support groups are readily available and easily accessible through community organizations, healthcare providers, religious institutions, or online platforms dedicated to specific topics or demographics. Whether meeting in person or virtually, these groups provide a valuable connection, validation, and support for individuals navigating the challenges of anticipatory grief. This accessibility ensures that no one must face these challenges alone.

Research has consistently demonstrated the significant benefits of peer support groups in helping individuals cope with anticipatory grief. For instance, a study published in the Journal of Palliative Medicine, a reputable peer-reviewed journal, highlighted the positive impact of participation in peer support groups. The study, conducted over a period of two years and involving a diverse group of caregivers, found that caregivers of older adults who engaged in such groups reported significant improvements in their emotional well-being. Specifically, participants experienced reduced feelings of isolation, which can often accompany the caregiving journey. Moreover, the study revealed that individuals who joined peer support groups felt a profound sense of empowerment, becoming better equipped to manage the challenges associated with caregiving. These findings underscore the importance of peer support networks in providing emotional solace and practical guidance to those navigating the complexities of anticipatory grief.

By accessing professional support through therapy and counseling and connecting with peer support groups and online communities, individuals and families facing anticipatory grief can find comfort, validation, and guidance. This guidance, coupled with the practical resources available, can help them feel empowered and equipped as they navigate the challenges of caregiving and grief. We encourage you to explore the resources mentioned in this article and consider joining a peer support group. This chapter aims to provide practical resources and support for individuals and families seeking assistance in coping with aging and grief's emotional, psychological, and practical aspects.

Embracing Aging:
A Natural Phase of Life

Embracing aging as a natural phase of life goes beyond merely accepting the passage of time; it fosters a positive outlook on the aging process and its associated transitions. The study published in the Journal of Gerontology: Psychological Sciences sheds light on the profound implications of such positive attitudes toward aging. According to the research findings, older adults with optimistic views about aging tended to exhibit superior physical health and cognitive functioning compared to their counterparts with negative attitudes. Moreover, the study revealed a compelling correlation between positive aging attitudes and longevity, suggesting that individuals who embraced aging with positivity tended to live longer lives. These findings underscore the powerful influence of mindset on aging experience, highlighting the importance of everyone's role in cultivating optimism and resilience as they age.

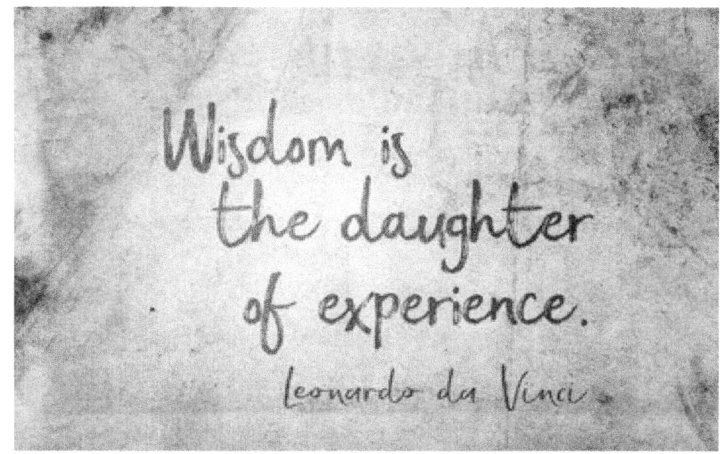

> Wisdom is the daughter of experience.
> leonardo da Vinci

Embracing the Wisdom and Experience of the Elderly

As individuals age, they accrue a wealth of wisdom and life experience, which can profoundly enrich their own lives and those of others. This wisdom and experience can manifest in various ways, such as the ability to navigate complex social situations, make sound decisions based on past experiences, and offer valuable advice. The significance of embracing this wisdom and experience lies not only in acknowledging its intrinsic value but also in recognizing its potential to contribute positively to relationships and communities. Studies in gerontology and psychology have provided compelling insights into the relationship between aging and well-being, shedding light on the factors that foster a fulfilling and meaningful later life.

The study published in the Journal of Gerontology, which surveyed a diverse sample of older and younger adults, revealed some fascinating insights. It found that older adults consistently reported higher life satisfaction levels than their younger counterparts. What's more, a staggering 80% of older adults expressed a strong sense of fulfillment and contentment with their lives. When asked about the factors contributing to their happiness, many older adults cited their sense of purpose, fulfillment, and interconnectedness with others. This underscores the active role that older adults play in shaping their own well-being, empowering them to take control of their happiness and fulfillment.

These statistics underscore the profound impact of embracing the wisdom and experience that come with age. By valuing the unique perspectives and insights of older adults, individuals, and communities can foster an environment that celebrates their contributions and nurtures their continued growth and well-being. This recognition of their contributions not only enriches their lives but also fosters a sense of appreciation and respect in the community, creating a more inclusive and supportive environment for all.

Finding Purpose:

Discovering Fulfillment in Caregiving

Caregiving roles present individuals with a profound opportunity for personal growth and self-fulfillment. By offering comfort, support, and assistance to aging parents, caregivers not only fulfill practical needs but also find deep purpose and meaning in their lives. Research has explored the impact of caregiving on individuals' well-being, revealing its potential to elevate life satisfaction and psychological health.

A significant study in the Journal of Aging and Health examined the experiences of caregivers of older adults, shedding light on the connection between caregiving roles and well-being. The study surveyed a diverse group of caregivers and non-caregivers, comparing their levels of life satisfaction and psychological well-being. The results were encouraging, showing that caregivers consistently reported higher levels of life satisfaction and psychological well-being than non-caregivers. A substantial majority of caregivers expressed a deep sense of fulfillment and contentment in their caregiving roles.

Moreover, when asked about the factors contributing to their happiness, caregivers frequently cited their sense of purpose and fulfillment derived from caregiving. Many caregivers, who were often adult children or close relatives, expressed a profound connection to their role, emphasizing the importance of providing care and support to their aging parents, who often had chronic health conditions or disabilities, as a source of meaning in their lives.

These findings underscore the transformative power of caregiving roles in fostering purpose and fulfillment. By recognizing and embracing the inherent value of caregiving, individuals can derive profound satisfaction and fulfillment from their roles as caregivers, enriching their lives and those they care for.

Finding Meaning in Providing Comfort to Aging Parents

Discovering the emotional depth in providing comfort and support to aging parents transcends the practical tasks of caregiving. It involves a profound understanding of the value and significance of caregiving roles and a willingness to create a positive impact in the lives of loved ones. Caregiving is not merely a series of tasks; it is a heartfelt expression of love, empathy, and commitment.

Extensive research has shed light on the intricate nature of caregiving roles and their influence on individuals' well-being. Caregivers of older adults often find themselves entangled in a complex array of responsibilities, from aiding with daily activities to providing emotional support and companionship. Despite the inherent challenges, many caregivers experience a profound sense of personal growth and fulfillment from their roles, offering a beacon of hope amidst the difficulties.

Research consistently reveals that caregivers of older adults often experience higher levels of life satisfaction and psychological well-being compared to non-caregivers. This is largely due to the profound sense of purpose and satisfaction that caregivers derive from their roles. By offering comfort, support, and assistance to aging parents, caregivers play a crucial part in their loved ones' lives, enhancing their well-being and quality of life.

Furthermore, caregivers often find significance in the reciprocal nature of caregiving, as the support they extend to their aging parents fortifies their bond and deepens their relationship. This sense of connection and intimacy fosters a profound sense of fulfillment and satisfaction, underscoring the mutual benefits of caregiving roles in the lives of caregivers and their loved ones.

Uncovering the transformative power in providing comfort and support to aging parents is a deeply personal journey. It involves acknowledging the inherent value of caregiving roles and embracing the chance to create a positive difference in the lives of loved ones, ultimately enriching both the caregiver's life and the lives of those they care for.

Building Resilience Through Mind Self-Compassion

Building resilience through mindfulness and self-compassion practices is not just essential, it's empowering. These practices equip us with the tools to navigate life's transitions and challenges with grace and strength. Mindfulness, the practice of being present and aware of one's thoughts, feelings, and sensations without judgment, cultivates emotional awareness and acceptance. Self-compassion, on the other hand, involves treating oneself with kindness and understanding, especially in times of difficulty or failure, empowering us to bounce back stronger.

Research has unequivocally shown that these practices can profoundly affect resilience and well-being. Mindfulness-based interventions, which often include practices such as meditation, deep breathing, and body scans, have been found to enhance resilience and reduce symptoms of stress, anxiety, and depression. The effectiveness of these interventions is not a matter of debate. For example, a meta-analysis published in the Journal of Consulting and Clinical Psychology demonstrated that mindfulness-based interventions effectively improved resilience and psychological well-being across various populations, including caregivers of older adults.

These findings underscore the practicality of incorporating mindfulness and self-compassion practices into daily life. It's not about adding more to our already busy schedules, but about making small, meaningful changes that can enhance resilience and cope effectively with life's challenges. By developing emotional awareness, self-acceptance, and adaptive coping skills, individuals can build the resilience needed to navigate transitions and adversities with greater ease and strength. Moreover, these practices offer caregivers of older adults valuable tools for managing the stress and emotional demands of caregiving, ultimately promoting their well-being and quality of life.

Embrace Flexibility and Adaptability in Change

Embracing flexibility and adaptability is not just a necessity for navigating life's inevitable transitions and challenges, but also a powerful tool that empowers us to face them with resilience and grace. It's about acknowledging that change is a natural part of life and learning to respond to it with openness and flexibility. Research consistently shows that individuals who possess the ability to adapt to life's transitions tend to experience better psychological well-being and overall quality of life, reinforcing the idea that we have the power to shape our own well-being.

A notable study published in the Journal of Personality and Social Psychology delved into the relationship between adaptability and well-being. The study found that individuals who demonstrated higher levels of adaptability not only coped better with life's uncertainties but also reported greater life satisfaction, happiness, and psychological well-being. These findings underscore the potential for positive change and growth that adaptability can bring, instilling a sense of hope and optimism in the face of challenges.

Be Kind To Yourself

Incorporating mindfulness and self-compassion into daily life is not just a practice, but a personal investment in our ability to adapt to life's transitions and challenges. Mindfulness practices, such as meditation and mindful breathing, cultivate awareness of the present moment and help us respond to stressors with greater clarity and calmness. Self-compassion, the practice of treating oneself with kindness and understanding, fosters resilience by promoting self-acceptance and emotional resilience in the face of adversity. These practices are not just tools, but a path to personal growth and well-being.

By incorporating mindfulness and self-compassion into daily life, individuals can enhance their ability to adapt to life's changes with greater ease and resilience. These practices provide valuable tools for navigating transitions, managing stress, and fostering emotional well-being, ultimately promoting greater fulfillment and quality of life.

Celebrating Legacy:

Honoring the Memories and Contributions of Aging Parents

Preserving Family History Through Storytelling and Documentation

Celebrating legacy involves more than just honoring the memories and contributions of aging parents; it also entails actively preserving family history through storytelling and documentation. While it may seem daunting at first, especially if you're unsure where to start or if your parents are reluctant to share, research indicates that such practices can profoundly affect familial bonds and individual well-being. Remember, it's not about the quantity of stories shared, but the quality of the connections they foster.

Reminiscence and storytelling are not just about preserving the past; they're about building bridges between generations. By sharing experiences and family narratives, individuals can strengthen their sense of identity and deepen their understanding of their family's history. These activities also promote intergenerational understanding and appreciation, bridging the gap between different age groups within the family and fostering a sense of belonging and unity.

Reminiscence and storytelling are not just about preserving family history; they're about promoting emotional fulfillment and resilience among older adults. A study published in the Journal of Gerontology: Psychological Sciences found that older adults who actively engaged in these activities reported significantly greater life satisfaction and psychological well-being. These findings underscore the importance of preserving family history and sharing stories as a means of promoting well-being among older adults, offering a reassuring and hopeful perspective.

By celebrating legacy through reminiscence and storytelling, families can create meaningful connections across generations and cultivate a sense of continuity and belonging. These practices not only honor the memories of aging parents but also contribute to the emotional well-being and cohesion of the entire family unit, including the younger generation who can learn valuable lessons and gain a deeper appreciation for their family's history.

The process of honoring aging parents' legacy is not just about acknowledging their contributions and accomplishments. It's a profound journey of actively commemorating their lives through meaningful acts of remembrance. This process holds immense importance as it helps us recognize the impact of our aging parents on our lives, regardless of any past difficulties or challenges in the relationship.

For those who have experienced strained or hurtful relationships with their aging parents, the process of honoring their legacy can be particularly intricate. It may require a journey of forgiveness, acceptance, and finding meaning in the shared experiences, both positive and negative. In this context, honoring means understanding the humanity and complexity of our parents' lives, recognizing their flaws and imperfections while also appreciating their strengths and achievements.

Research strongly suggests that engaging in acts of remembrance can be profoundly healing and transformative for individuals and families navigating the grief of losing a loved one. Memorialization rituals and traditions provide a powerful opportunity to celebrate the deceased's life, preserve their memory, and find deep solace in the collective support of family and friends.

A study published in the Journal of Loss and Trauma delved into the therapeutic benefits of memorialization rituals. The research found that these rituals can facilitate the grieving process by providing a sense of closure, comfort, and connection. Furthermore, memorialization promoted healing and resilience in the face of loss, helping individuals and families navigate the complexities of grief with greater strength and resilience.

By actively honoring the legacy of aging parents through acts of remembrance, individuals can find profound healing, closure, and a deep sense of connection to their loved ones. These rituals serve as a powerful testament to the enduring impact of our parents' lives and provide a deeply meaningful way to carry forward their memories for generations to come.

Reflecting on the Journey:
Acknowledging Growth and Healing

Recognizing Personal Growth and Resilience Throughout the Grieving Process

As we reach the end of this transformative journey, it's crucial to pause and reflect on the significant personal growth and resilience that unfolds during the grieving process. Extensive research has illuminated how individuals undergo profound transformations and discover newfound inner strengths after experiencing loss. This journey of grief often leads to unexpected insights and revelations, shaping individuals in ways they never thought possible.

A study featured in the Journal of Traumatic Stress delved into the phenomenon of personal growth following traumatic loss. The research revealed that individuals who confronted traumatic loss reported experiencing remarkable levels of personal growth and resilience. These individuals exhibited heightened levels of self-awareness, gaining a deeper understanding of themselves and their place in the world. Additionally, they displayed increased empathy, cultivating a greater capacity for understanding and compassion toward others experiencing hardship or loss. Moreover, they developed a profound appreciation for life, recognizing each moment's preciousness and cherishing the beauty and resilience inherent in the human experience. These positive outcomes of personal growth and resilience offer a beacon of optimism for those navigating the journey of grief.

Through the journey of grief, individuals not only navigate the pain and sorrow of loss but also embark on a path of self-discovery and transformation. This process of personal growth is often characterized by resilience, as individuals harness their inner resources to navigate adversity and emerge stronger and more resilient than before. As we reflect on our own journey of grief, let us not forget to acknowledge the profound resilience and personal growth that has emerged from the depths of sorrow and loss.

Acknowledge Self-Reflection and Healing

Understanding the importance of self-reflection and healing is crucial when it comes to navigating the complex landscape of anticipatory grief. Taking the time to explore our emotions, seek support from loved ones, and prioritize self-care can significantly aid in our healing process. These practices can help us find meaning in the midst of our loss, offering a beacon of hope in our darkest moments.

Extensive research underscores the therapeutic benefits of self-reflection and healing modalities, such as journaling, meditation, and therapy. These practices can provide a sense of relief and comfort, bolstering emotional well-being and fostering resilience when confronting adversity. Notably, a study featured in the Journal of Counseling Psychology delved into the impact of such practices on individuals grappling with grief. The findings revealed that individuals who actively engaged in self-reflection and healing practices reported significantly higher psychological well-being and life satisfaction levels than those who did not.

By embracing self-reflection and healing, we can navigate the ups and downs of anticipatory grief with greater resilience and understanding. This journey can lead to profound personal growth and transformation, even in the face of the most challenging losses. It is through these practices that we can find strength and resilience, and ultimately, discover a new sense of self amidst the pain.

Hope for the Future Despite Loss and Change

As we gaze towards the horizon of the unknown, nurturing hope and optimism becomes an indispensable compass guiding us through the labyrinth of loss and transformation. Consider the stories of the following, who despite the formidable challenges that loss and change presented, cultivated a steadfast sense of hope and optimism that served as a beacon of light amidst the shadows of uncertainty.

- **Anne Frank**: Despite enduring the horrors of the Holocaust and living in seclusion for two years, Anne Frank's unwavering hope and optimism, as reflected in her writings, continue to resonate and inspire people worldwide. Her diary, a testament to love, humanity, and the beauty of life, stands as a beacon of resilience and hope.
- **Nelson Mandela**: Imprisoned for 27 years due to his anti-apartheid activism, Nelson Mandela emerged as a beacon of forgiveness and reconciliation that steered South Africa towards democracy. His unyielding belief in the power of unity and equality, a belief that still resonates today, continues to inspire generations.
- **Malala Yousafzai**: Malala Yousafzai's journey is a testament to the power of resilience. After surviving an assassination attempt by the Taliban for advocating girls' education, she transformed into a global symbol of courage. Her fight for all children's educational rights is a testament to her unwavering determination.
- **Stephen Hawking**: Diagnosed with amyotrophic lateral sclerosis (ALS) at the age of 21, Stephen Hawking defied the odds by continuing his groundbreaking work in theoretical physics. His resilience and determination to

unlock the mysteries of the universe inspired millions worldwide.

- **Maya Angelou**: Overcoming a traumatic childhood and racial discrimination, Maya Angelou became a celebrated poet, author, and civil rights activist. Her words of wisdom and resilience, expressed through influential works like "Still I Rise," continue to uplift and empower people facing adversity.

An extensive body of research, including a seminal study featured in the Journal of Positive Psychology, underscores the transformative power of hope and optimism on individuals' psychological well-being and overall quality of life, especially in the face of adversity. The findings of this study provide a reassuring and confident illumination that individuals who steadfastly held onto hope and optimism reported elevated levels of happiness, life satisfaction, and resilience compared to those trapped in hopelessness and despair.

By embracing hope and optimism, we not only fortify our resilience but also cultivate a mindset that is primed for personal growth and renewal. This empowerment allows us to navigate the turbulent seas of loss with courage and unwavering determination.

Embrace Opportunities for Growth and Connection

Embracing the journey of growth and connection as we move forward beckons us to acknowledge the transformative potential inherent in the aftermath of loss. The research underscores the profound shifts and metamorphoses that individuals, in their remarkable resilience, often undergo in the wake of grief, revealing pathways to personal and relational evolution that transcends the pain of loss.

Studies have illuminated the kaleidoscope of transformations that unfold following loss, unveiling a tapestry woven with threads of compassion, empathy, and a newfound reverence for life. These shifts in perspective serve as catalysts for profound inner growth, fostering a deeper understanding of the human experience and our interconnectedness with others.

By embracing opportunities for growth and connection, we embark on a journey of self-discovery and renewal. One practical way to do this is by journaling your thoughts and feelings. This can help you find solace and purpose amidst the ebb and flow of grief. Through this journey, we cultivate deeper connections with ourselves as we navigate the labyrinth of emotions, nurturing a sense of resilience and self-compassion that sustains us through the darkest of days.

Moreover, embracing growth and connection extends beyond the boundaries of the self, inviting us to forge deeper bonds with our loved ones and communities. Through compassion, support, and shared vulnerability, we weave a tapestry of interconnectedness that transcends the barriers of loss, fostering a sense of belonging and solidarity that nurtures our collective healing. In this shared journey, no one is alone.

By embracing opportunities for growth and connection, we honor the complexities of the human experience, finding beauty and meaning amidst the tapestry of grief and loss. Through these profound connections, we illuminate the path forward, guided by the light of resilience, compassion, and the enduring power of the human spirit. This journey is for all of us, regardless of our backgrounds or experiences.

Closing Thoughts:

Navigating Anticipatory Grief with Grace and Understanding

As we near the end of our journey, it becomes increasingly evident that grief and loss are profound experiences that defy simple categorization. Anticipatory grief, a term used to describe the grief experienced before a loss, adds layers of complexity to the emotional landscape as individuals grapple with the impending loss of a loved one. This multifaceted journey encompasses a broad spectrum of emotions, ranging from profound sadness and anxiety to moments of hope and resilience.

Understanding the complexity of anticipatory grief is crucial for fostering empathy and understanding among individuals on this path. Each person's experience of grief is unique, shaped by their relationship with the aging parent, their personal coping mechanisms, and their cultural and societal influences. This uniqueness is not a barrier, but a bridge, connecting us in our shared experiences of grief and loss.

Approaching grief with compassion involves acknowledging the full range of accompanying emotions without judgment or expectation. It means offering a listening ear, a comforting presence, and a willingness to sit with the discomfort and uncertainty that grief brings. Research has shown that compassionate support is not just a gesture, but a lifeline, significantly easing the burden of grief, reducing feelings of isolation, and promoting healing and resilience.

Moreover, understanding the nuanced nature of grief allows us to tailor our support to meet the diverse needs of individuals navigating this journey. Whether through acts of kindness, encouragement or simply being there for someone in their time of need, we can create a supportive environment where grief is honored, and healing can occur. As we conclude our journey, let us carry forward this spirit of compassion and understanding, knowing that it can transform grief into a journey of growth, resilience, and, ultimately, healing.

As we conclude our journey, it's imperative to emphasize the ongoing need for dialogue and support regarding aging and grief in our communities and society. By fostering open and honest conversations about these crucial topics, we can dismantle barriers, challenge stigma, and cultivate a culture of compassion and understanding.

Continued dialogue around aging and grief allows us to confront societal taboos and misconceptions head-on. By sharing personal stories, experiences, and insights, we can illuminate the realities of aging and the complexities of grief, fostering a deep sense of empathy and connection among individuals from all walks of life. These stories, filled with raw emotions and shared experiences, have the power to unite us and empower individuals to navigate these issues with greater understanding and sensitivity through education and awareness-raising initiatives.

Our commitment to one another's well-being is not just a statement. It's a commitment we demonstrate by providing ongoing support to those grappling with aging, grief, and loss. Whether through support groups, community outreach programs, or simply offering a listening ear to a friend or neighbor in need, we can create spaces of empathy, kindness, and grace. These are the spaces where individuals feel seen, heard, and valued, and where our collective strength shines through.

As we venture forward on our individual paths, let us do so not just with grace, understanding, and compassion, but with the knowledge that we are not alone in our experiences. We are a community, and together, with strength and resilience, we can face whatever challenges may come our way. We can navigate the complexities of aging, grief, and loss with dignity and grace, knowing that we have each other's backs.

Printed in Great Britain
by Amazon